D0527642

WITHDRAWN
FROM STOCK

Pete Doherty
the shambolic libertine

Evesham & Malvern Hills College
Library

34082

Deadications...

Pete Doherty, Kate Moss, the **Daily Mirror**, the **News of the World**...

Ta to...

Valentina, who made the book possible

Supriya, who made it look much better than I wrote it

Sophie, who made me use the facts she'd researched rather than
those I invented

Lucky, Artnik's golden retriever, who made up for being indentured
to a contract that gave me all the rights of a word-slave

First published in Great Britain in 2005
by Artnik
Revised Edition 2006
by Artnik an imprint of Linveco AG
London Office:
 Queenstown Road
London SW8 4LH
UK

© **Artnik 2005**
© **Linveco AG 2006**

All rights reserved. No part of this publication may be reproduced, stored in or
introduced into a retrieval system, or transmitted in any form or by any means
(electronic, mechanical, photocopying, recording or otherwise) without the prior
written permission of both the copyright owner and the publisher of this book.

ISBN 1-903906-74-1

Design: Supriya Sahai
Pictures: Live Photography
Pictures: Justin Thomas
Book Concept: Nicholas Artsrunik
Editor: John McVicar
Reseach: Sophie Gregson

Printed and bound in Croatia
by HG—Consulting

Pete Doherty
the shambolic libertine

SEAMUS CRAIC

EVESHAM COLLEGE
782
LIBRARY
34082

artnik books

A 'TIME FOR HEROES'?

Society generally gets the heroes it deserves, but sometimes it gets the heroes it doesn't ask for.

Our taste in popular music is there in the Top 40 for all to see: happy house, hip-hop, r'n'b, boybands, reality show contestants...

Yet both the public and mass media love the fact that just under the surface there are sounds which scream to our dark side. It's etched in the history of the UK charts - but these forces are reflected in society as much as in music. Whether it's the **Daily Mail** or the producers of **Newsnight**, the Chris de Burgh fan or Disgusted of Tunbridge Wells, they need Peter Doherty as much as the **NME** and the 14-year-old with his first guitar.

Sure, for those willing to see it, there is plenty enough that is dark and seditious about the very blandest the charts have to offer: the exploitation of naïve 'talent' by big business; the sexualising of pre-teens; the rampant libido of clean-cut idols and the hypocrisy of their management; the naked materialism of Bling and the underbelly of violence in urban pop.

But barring the occasional middle-class scare story about rap music and gun crime, this stuff doesn't exactly set the columns on fire. It's too unseemly. It's not what the doting grannies who buy these records for their little angels want to hear. It throws into question fundamental consumer values, like who are the good guys and who are the bad guys. The moral corruption in pop is all there, it is not salubrious but nor is it glamorous... in short, IT'S NOT WHAT WE LIKE TO CALL ROCK 'N' ROLL.

Even when guitar music hasn't dominated the cultural agenda, we've always found room for the concept of rock as rebellion. It didn't matter if Englebert Humperdinck began to outsell the Stones, the band which represented the threat to society were still the band getting the column inches. The Sex Pistols only made one record but it put youth culture back on the front pages after a decade of soft-rock and concept albums. And Liam Gallagher aped around and spat and swore, and suddenly from a loved-up, dance-obsessed music scene the 90s had a dirty rock idol: a composite of all our favourite drug-addled bad-boys, living out a new lad fantasy to meet the spirit of the age.

PETE DOHERTY IS DIFFERENT - which is not to say he doesn't fit a pattern. Like the Stones, the Pistols and Oasis, his band The Libertines conquered the charts on the back of controversy. In musical terms, comparisons to those bands may be lazy and toothless, with his group owing more to the whimsical side of English punk - The Jam and The Buzzcocks, the angry intelligence of The Clash - or the Albion cabaret of The Kinks. It is principally as a tabloid cause célèbre Pete Doherty appears to have inherited a mantle from the great rock antiheroes. Sadly, since we cannot view Doherty's life in isolation from his image, these more superficial comparisons are as instructive as the musical ones.

There are similarities, too, in the manner of their breakthrough - shock and awe, you might say. Despite coming across as cult outsiders, hysterical mass-media coverage early in their career drove all these acts to the top of the charts.[1] They managed to hit the very summit at a time when wider society seemed to be protesting that it just wasn't ready for them.

'eart pours and shine'
out
The suckling attraction
from my 'rists to my ie'be
Tidal's my va'ers
a'rag queen in underflow
enile streaming vu'sa
                  steaming   !'

Of course, it was this very infamy and outrage that fuelled the fire; but where the management of the Stones or the Pistols had harnessed the ill-will cynically for self-promotion ('Would You Let Your Daughter Go Out With A Rolling Stone?'), and where the Gallaghers were pantomime villains who not-so-secretly enjoyed the blessing of the bored red-top editors, The Libertines seemed caught up in an image that rapidly got too big for them to handle. They were happy to promulgate the impression of all-out decadence - after all, it was nothing more than the truth - but you cannot control the PR of someone who cannot control himself. The fans loved Pete because he was real, but his problems were too real for either his bandmates or his reputation at large. If we can put ourselves in the mindset of **The Sun** for a moment: the British public loves a bad boy, but junkies are scum.

And this is perhaps where Doherty is most different - if not from history's great rock and roll casualties, then certainly from all the other pin-ups who occupy the gossip pages.[2] It's something as simple, as stupid, as superficial as drug choice. We can handle cocaine, it's become just another word for money. Soft drugs are fun, even acid is 'creative'. Binge drinking is as common now in office parties as it used to be at aftershows. But heroin and crack cocaine, those guys we still can't get our heads round. They sound like poverty and crime and AIDS.

HOW CAN WE LOOK UP TO SOMEONE WHOSE HABITS ARE THE SAME AS THE PEOPLE WE LOOK DOWN ON IN THE STREETS?

Well, it helps if they're stepping out with a supermodel.

By all accounts a choirboy geek with a love of
poetry and football, the young Pete Doherty
only got to meet the doyens of Camden cool
through his older sister's mates - like big
brother figure Carl Barat, who taught him his
first guitar chords. After six months of Carl
telling him he was shit, they decided to form
a band together. But this book is not
concerned with the generic early years.

THE BREAKTHROUGH

For those convinced that Doherty only made a success of his band on the
back of a drugs habit and celebrity girlfriend, it may surprise them to
know that The Libertines were signed to Rough Trade as early as
Christmas 2001 - that's three years before he met Kate Moss, 18 months
before his first arrest, and almost 9 months before his first reported
drug-fuelled fall-out.

Rough Trade was a forward-thinking label with a foot in the past. It was
formed at the height of UK punk by Geoff Travis, whose Rough Trade
record shop (established in 1976) was so popular with young bands that
within two years he was putting out their records himself. It soon built
a reputation as THE cult post-punk label, although its greatest success
came in the mid-80s with the more lyrical, strangely poppy sound of The
Smiths. While at the time it felt like a surprise change in direction
for the label, this collision of DIY punk values with intelligent
English whimsy does seem to embody the two sides of The Libertines.

Members of the band have indeed cited Morrissey as a
key influence. Rough Trade A&R man James Endeacott
said the label's soul could be found in the 'TIME
IN THE MID-80S WHEN NEW WAVE MUSIC
CROSSED OVER TO THE MAINSTREAM'3, and so
The Libertines had found the perfect home to make
their own transition from punk hopefuls to
mainstream success.

Among their new labelmates they found The Strokes, the punk revivalists
du jour and another act who sometimes sounded like their record
collections. The band would come to endure invidious comparison with the
well-bred New Yorkers - a comparison initially intended as a compliment,
both to their dress-sense and their sound, but ultimately in a way that
only serves to warn us of the disposability of retro fashion. Even
though The Strokes stayed together while The Libertines imploded, it is
the latter band whose presence is more keenly felt on the British music
scene today.

Still, at the time 'The British Strokes' was about the greatest
compliment a music journalist could muster, so as a badge to wear it
served them well enough. They supported their more senior labelmates on
two rescheduled dates in February 2002, and this served as a springboard
to some dates with The Vines and full-on **NME** endorsement. On May 14th
of that year they were asked to headline the weekly rag's inaugural
'Bring It On' night, to fete the launch of their free national gig
listings paper. Among the crowd at 93 Feet East in London's Brick Lane
were various liggers and taste-setters: journalists, support act The
Eighties Matchbox B-Line Disaster, The Charlatans' Tim Burgess... and one
Jefferson Hack, editor of **Dazed & Confused** magazine but probably then
more widely known as the lesser half of supermodel Kate Moss.

'NOBODY WE'VE SIGNED IS OUT TO MAKE A LOT OF MONEY AND GET ON TV. NOTHING IS MANUFACTURED LIKE THAT, WE HAVEN'T GOT ANY FAME-HUNGRY PEOPLE. WE'VE GOT PEOPLE WHO LIKE FAME BUT THEY DON'T GRASP AND STRIVE FOR IT,'

insisted Endeacott of his new signings at
Rough Trade. Sadly reflected fame
is often the curse of those who
choose to stand close to the
stars, and the grasping love of
money usually cited in whispers as
the reason why. Pete would
discover this in time.

All agreed the debut single had to be 'What A Waster'. Punchy,
funny, full of cockney slang like 'divvy' and 'two-bob cunt',
Endeacott knew it would get zero radio play but felt it would
issue an unfettered statement of intent. He was right about that
part, but hadn't expected Mark and Lard to make it single of the
week anyway (albeit heavily 'bleeped'). Bernard Butler's
production was a little mannered, a little Suede, even, on the
guitars - so much so that Doherty later claimed he couldn't
listen to it on hearing the opening bars, so far was it from his
intention. However, despite the personality clash, and allegedly
the blows, all parties take credit for a great debut record. The
launch party at Virgin Megastore kicked off in appropriate
fashion, the band nicking copies of their own CD off the shelves
to hand out to friends.

Setting a pattern for the rest of their short career, the first
single was rapidly followed by the first fall-out - in public, at
least. The title of 'What A Waster' was already providing
headline writers with the kind of hook they needed, though at the
time it seemed to refer more to wasted nights out than wasted
talent. The fisticuffs between Pete Doherty and Carl Barat was
presented as a bit of fun, a little bit of rock 'n' roll spice in
a world of Travis and Coldplay rather than a serious sign of
mental disturbance - even though it ended here with a punch in
the throat and a knee to the head. Normally when a band are
reported as 'fighting' in the studio, it means one person
deciding their guitar parts had been turned down and quietly
sulking for a couple of days. Here, during the early album mixes,
a drunken 6am playfight escalated into a vicious brawl - after
which Pete, nursing Carl's retaliatory knee-print in his temple,
staggered out into the night cursing his bandmate and would not
be seen for 48 hours.

The main problem there was the band's show at the Scarborough
Festival, scheduled for later that day (August 3rd). In the end,
with Doherty uncontactable and in any case persona non grata, the
band had to perform as a three-piece.

Barat had his revenge that evening, casually announcing that he'd had a fight with his best mate before introducing, obviously enough, 'What A Waster'. The band remained tight-lipped about what provoked Doherty to lash out suddenly, but from Carl's impassioned rendering of 'What a fucking waster/You pissed it all up the wall', he left little doubt as to who was to blame - not for anyone in the audience that night.

Still, it was already clear that there might be more tensions brewing. Although a spokesman released the first of what would be many statements having to deny any split, when the band did reconvene in the studio later in the week they would have been surprised to read the manner in which the NME covered the story. 'Frontman PETE DOHERTY went AWOL following a studio bust-up with guitarist CARL BARAT,' read the first line, and the article went on to suggest that by 'kneeing his singer in the head' Carl had committed some act of insubordination.

The Libertines were nothing if not a gang, and to imply some kind of feudal system was not going to go down well in the camp. Barat was no mere 'guitarist' to Doherty's frontman, the two duelled lead vocals like an angry face-off at an open-mike night and Barat, as co-songwriter, can't have enjoyed reports that he had to 'learn' his own songs in the bus on the way to the show. This was no mere karaoke performance, this was a version of The Libertines that live fans were going to have to get used to - one without the angel-faced urchin they'd seen on the poster.

STILL, EVEN IN THAT MIS-PRINT IT WAS ESTABLISHED FROM EARLY ON WHICH MEMBER THE PRESS WERE INSTINCTIVELY DRAWN TO AS THE CHARISMATIC HEART OF THE BAND.[4]

The cut that had caused all the trouble was 'Up The Bracket', the title track from the forthcoming album already earmarked as their next single. It took intervention from a man they could really respect to get the song, and the band, back on track. That man was the legendary Mick Jones of The Clash. Not only did he have the best possible qualifications for dealing with an

intelligent London punk band, he also had experience with the politics of sharing the limelight. He had co-written most of The Clash's material with Joe Strummer, but while his more visible bandmate was considered the frontman, he also did his share of singing - getting his most famous payday with the lead vocal on their only No.1 single, 'Should I Stay Or Should I Go'.

Rough Trade made the inspired decision of roping in Jones after a mutual friend alerted both parties they were working just round the corner from each other. 'They sent me a CD of their stuff and I thought it was really good - otherwise I wouldn't have done it,' Jones told the **NME** at the time.[5] Although the mutual appreciation society didn't take long to kick in - the band would later come on stage to the classic 'London Calling' - amazingly The Libertines didn't know much more about Mick Jones than he knew about The Libertines. 'He just turned up in the studio and within half an hour he had a "What A Waster" badge on and was drinking a can of lager. We didn't know much about him,' admitted Pete. 'But over the last few weeks we've been listening to lots of The Clash!'

If the band weren't too familiar with The Clash's output
before the decisive sessions for the Up The Bracket album,
then it shows quite what an influence that time spent with
Mick Jones must have had. From the vocal styling to the
lyrics to the guitar sound, at times the similarity to The
Clash's first record was uncanny. In key single 'Time For
Heroes' especially, the band rode that same rocky ride of
cut-up rhythms and slurred-but-catchy vocals, at once lazy
but angry. Jones admitted the sense of déjà vu but was
careful not to lay it on too heavy. 'They do remind me of
The Clash a little bit,' he said. 'They're a London rock
'n' roll group, which obviously appeals to me. They're
very good lyrically too. There are the same elements, you
know - four guys in the band, the tunes are really good,
you can't help but get sucked in.'

The album was packed with terrace anthems, like the
singalong 'Boys In The Band', but the style wasn't
football hooligan - despite Pete's childhood love of QPR.
Instead critics were taken with the band's allusion to
some strange Arcadian neverland, intrigued by the elusive
nature of this 'other country' Albion. The impression of
harking back to a golden age was enhanced by the iconic
choice of redcoat military jackets for the key album
photoshoots, an idea - like the band's name itself - which
all parties now insist they came up with. While they liked
the imagery, no journalist ever really gave much thought
to where this conceit was coming from or to divining what
Albion actually meant to Pete.

The fans did, though - at least, they thought they did, and that was the point. It was an escape, a dream, a mythical gilded retreat from grim reality. It could mean what you wanted to mean, as long as it gave you a flight of fancy, a temporary out from your miserable life.

Through drugs Pete ever existed in a hazy parallel world that looked like Britain but felt a world away. But he was searching for Arcadia, a place where none of this shit was necessary, a return to a golden state. Hence the Camden flat he and Carl shared, the venue for a hundred guerrilla gigs that started a whole new scene, became THE ALBION ROOMS: A GRUBBY DIVE THAT SEEMED TO THEM SOMEHOW MAGICAL AND PAVED WITH GOLD.

Of course, given the vagueness of these ideas, it helped that his oblique lyrical style gave the impression of him being off on his own - unsullied, inscrutable, sailing a good ship somewhere far away under his own wind.

Still, the goodwill towards the band from fellow professionals didn't last too long. The nationwide tour in October became a matter of infamy, which alienated their crew and their promoters but enshrined them as the stuff of teen legend. The closing night of the tour should have been a time for celebration and reflection, as they released their debut album to acclaim and went Top 30 in the singles chart with the title track... well, they managed the celebration at least, largely thanks to a six-figure publishing deal.

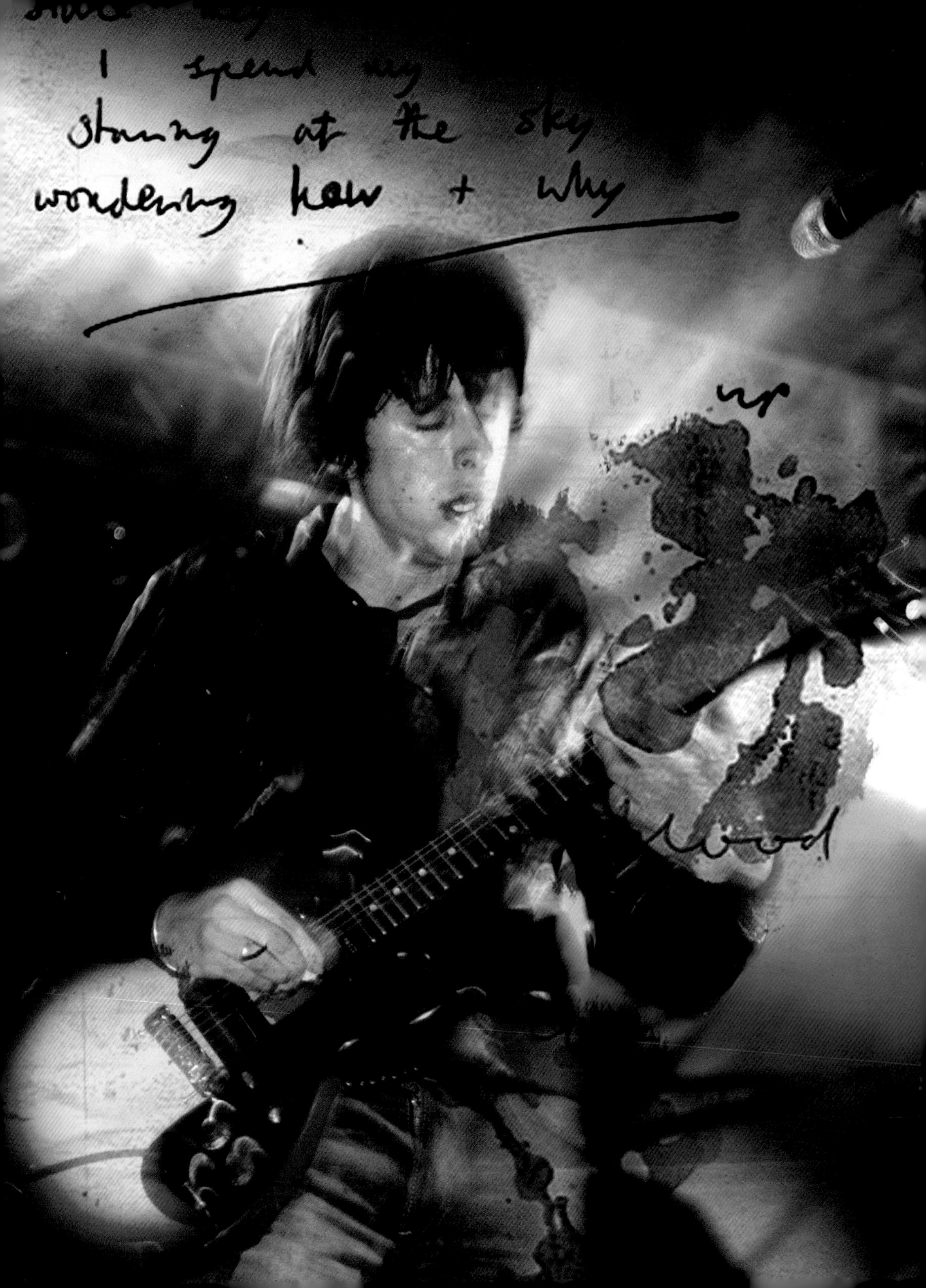

I spend my
staring at the sky
wondering how + why

Perhaps we need a little background here. A publishing
advance tends to be the first really exciting, sizeable sum
of money a young songwriter receives - unlike a recording
advance, it's not split all ways with the rest of the band,
and it's not held back by record company considerations
like studio costs, tour support and overheads. Pete and
Carl obviously didn't think it fair that the £400,000
they'd just received for a stake in their 'intellectual
property' from Sanctuary's publishing wing shouldn't be
shared around a little bit: how else can you explain an
outlay of ten grand on one massive end-of-tour bender?

Their behaviour so sickened their sound man that he'd
already walked out come the London show. But their tour
manager, well, he'd been doing bands for two decades and
seen some pretty wild times... surely he could ride out the
storm? Apparently not. After a month of groupies, drug and
alcohol binges, trouble with locals, fights with strangers
AND fights with each other, the old pro finally decided to
try and reel them in. The result? Sacked - for being 'too
strict'. A band insider admitted, 'The tour manager is a
really nice bloke. But he runs a tight ship, which didn't
go down well with Carl and Pete. He's been doing it for 22
years and he said he hadn't seen anything as bad. It was
debauchery.' Oh, and there was room for one final point-
scoring opportunity: 'He said that, in comparison, The
Strokes were pussycats.' At the time the comment seemed to
show the band were still in hock to their more established
labelmates, but in retrospect it is hard not to see it as a
sign that the credibility was swinging away from the posh
boys and towards something like the real thing.

The NME celebrated what they called 'one of the most
debauched tours in recent rock history' by giving the band
their first cover - decked out in their iconic red military
jackets. Their show at the West End's 100 Club received
rapturous notices for its intensity, sweat and - frankly -
bravery, after somehow making it through the marathon bender.
The frontmen were 'visibly weary', according to witnesses,
after 22 dates spent trying to
outdo each other on the road.
Soon enough, Carl would tire of
having to keep up with his
bandmate's terrifying capacity
for self-destruction.

Rumours soon went round fansites
that The Libertines needed a new
manager, in the mistaken belief
that the person sacked was acting
band manager Banny Poostchi (a
role later to be taken on by
Creation Records titan Alan
McGee). The web-boards were soon
clogged with offers to take on what sounded to thousands of
teenagers like the best job in the world. This kind of
colossal web-based community is what helped drive the band on
in the early days. 'They've found a way round the music
business,' is how McGee later put it. 'It's very web-based.
We put a message up on one of the Libertines messageboards
saying they were playing the Forum and suddenly we sold 5,500
tickets.' Speaking on his own Poptones website in 2004 after
the split, he reflected: 'The Libertines proved that you
didn't need the backing of the media, a major record label
deal and loads of money to be massive.'

The thing is, in their own strange way they did have the backing of the media: not just the acclaim of the weekly trendsetter NME, and the cautious approval of the 'grown-up' rock critics, but most crucially - and most fatally - the willingness of the mainstream media to get involved, and to condemn. Although stories of rock n' roll excess were commonplace, eyebrows were being raised even at this early stage by the sheer volume of the debauchery - and the then-unique love/hate relation-ship apparently enjoyed by the two singers, in a way that harkened back to the tabloid glory days of the Gallaghers. When McGee said, 'They're as vital as Oasis were in the '90s,' he meant culturally, musically, vital to the kids and to the industry... but where he was most right, unfortunately, was in how vital they were to the national press. There was a void in their gossip columns since Oasis had grown old and dull, and this new gang of brothers at war looked ripe to fill it; Peter Doherty in particular seemed to be the one they had their eye on. It was an unhappy relationship between pressman and poet which would blow up in both their faces.

Already the cracks were growing so alarmingly that PR-friendly rumours of wild unpredictability and rock 'n' roll behaviour were rapidly giving way to the very real prospect that the newly-broken band of 2003 might not even make it through to another album.

The pity of all this was the band were really starting to show their class. The single release of the anthemic 'Time For Heroes' at the beginning of 2003 showed the world how they could afford to leave a song of the destructive impact of 'What A Waster' off their debut LP. What's more, the growing critical reputation of Up The Bracket was beginning to be noticed across the Atlantic.

The US release of the album in March was a low-key
affair, as Brit debuts tend to be, but the college-radio
buzz fuelled by fashionable Stateside devotees of the UK
music papers meant that their first US appearance, at the
Coachella festival in New York, was highly anticipated.
NYC tends to be closer in taste to the UK and London
scene than the rest of the States: the likes of Blur and
Gomez were also appearing at the festival, which was
acting as a kind of showcase for British talent.

The Libertines, however, were the 'must-see' band - at
least, that was the cliché used by all the webloggers and
fansite reviewers eager to get a first glimpse.

WHETHER THEY WERE ANTICIPATING A TRIUMPH OR A CAR-CRASH, THEY WEREN'T TO BE DISAPPOINTED ON EITHER COUNT.

The scheduled show on Day 1 fulfilled all the voyeuristic
needs of those who had flocked to the stage fuelled by
rumours of drunkenness and disaster. Carl opened up by
spraying the crowd with champagne, but they had barely
played two songs before Pete threw the mike at the crowd
in an angry strop before the band walked off. The
audience didn't quite know how to react; drummer Gary
Powell blamed 'the fucked-up amp', but what the angrier
elements in the crowd didn't realise is that the blame
lay with previous act Ladytron, who'd spent so long
getting their act together beforehand that for once The
Libertines were suffering from somebody else's antisocial
behaviour.

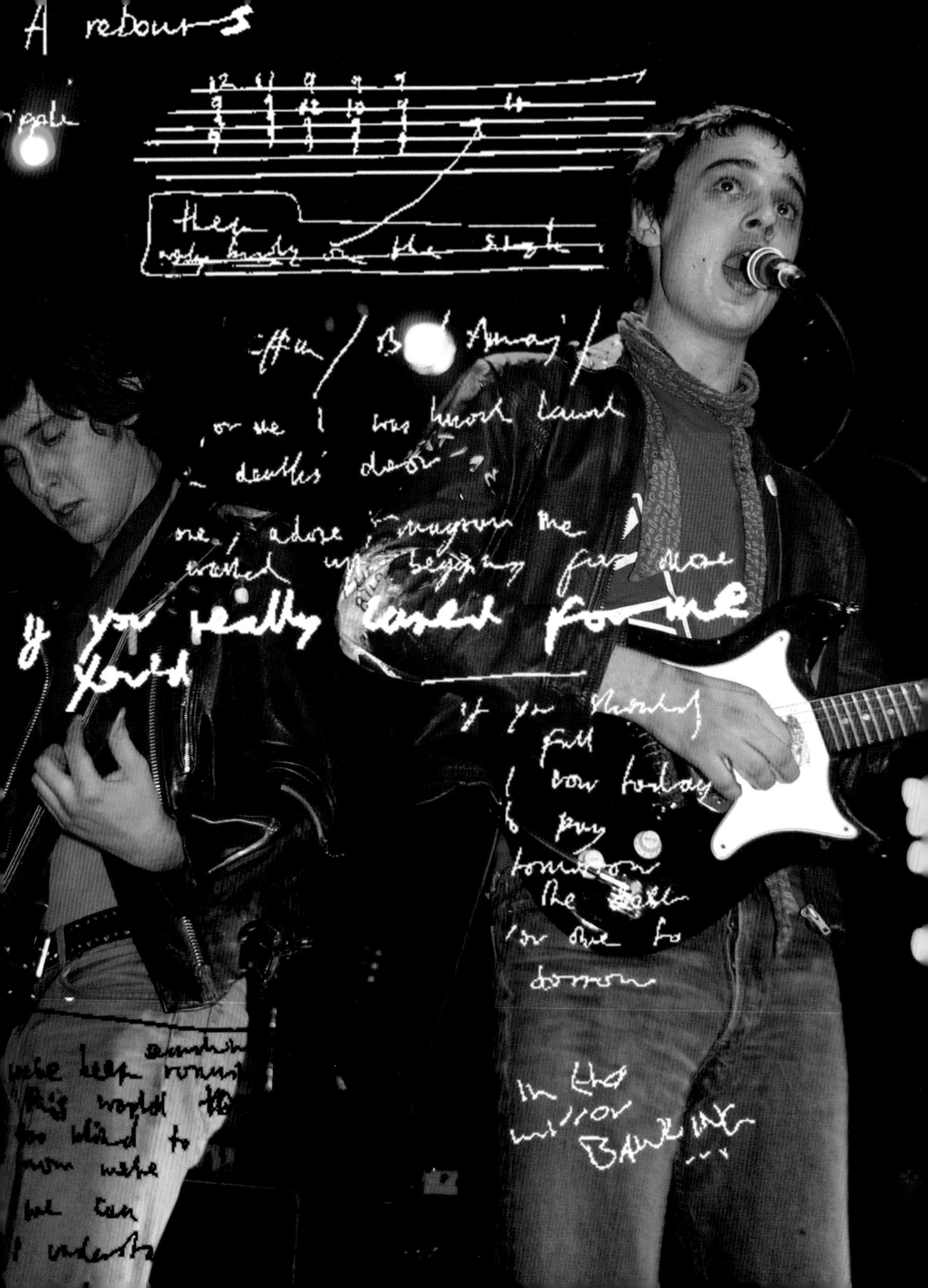
A rebours
If you really loved for me
in the mirror
BARKING

Fortunately the disquiet of the punters didn't go unnoticed by
the festival organisers, who hastily arranged to slot the band
in the next day. On the Sunday The Libertines had a chance to
do the one thing they could do even better than causing chaos -
a whole set of scrappy, poppy, stroppy songs about being
English. And it worked, too, delighting an American crowd for
the first time. Traditionally the US tour demands a higher level
of technical competence than the average Brit can deal with; but
just as had happened back home, here the rough edges only added
to the band's virtuoso levels of charm.

> 'KINDA-SLOPPY-ON-PURPOSE,' mused one
> reviewer. 'MISSED NOTES AND OUT-OF-TUNE
> GUITARS ACTUALLY ENHANCE THE PERFORMANCES.'[6]

In fairness to the British gig-goer, the fluffed notes and
scrappy style hadn't gone unnoticed over here. 'Like the whole
of the debut album, it's as rough and scruffy as a rag-and-bone
man's dog,' was how the *NME* reacted to the 'Time For Heroes'
single. 'We suspect that even when The Libs fall off a bar-stool
and smash all their teeth out on the floor, they do it with a
certain elegance.' Ex-*NME* photographer Roger Sargent,
responsible for their very first shoot, describes the lads'
winning magnetism:

'I could see they looked like an iconic band even before they
were famous. Every time I clicked the shutter it was like, wow,
that's an amazing moment.' He witnessed first-hand how such
innate cool helped win over the kids in America: 'The American
crowd really took to them. The Libertines are quintessentially
English, and for some reason the Americans like it.'[7]

Papelaria Luso-Brasileira
Abel d'Oliveira, L.ᵈᵃ
PAPELARIA, TIPOGRAFIA E ENCADERNAÇÃO
R. dos Correeiros, 14, 1.º - LISBOA
Telef. 2 5435
Para aquisição de um novo livro
dêste modelo basta indicar
a Referência N.º 90

CARE INSTRUCTIONS
MACHINE WASH 40°
INSIDE OUT WITH
LIKE COLOURS
IRON ON REVERSE

It was indeed strange that the Yanks seemed to take
to the very thing that had held back The Libertines'
idols, The Kinks, across the pond - namely the
quirky, cheeky sense of Little England as an island
against the world. But then it was never that
simple. It's worth bearing in mind that Ray Davis
only turned his pen to songs about the village
cricket green after an ugly promotional dispute had
led to them being black-balled in the States. Until
then the band's powerful riff-led pop had begun to
make an impression over there, and now The Libertines
had a chance to right that wrong - if only they would
stay together long enough to take it.

Already they'd had to cancel a European tour planned
for February due to the kind of 'illness' that
Libertines fans would have to get used to - an
infection called Pete Doherty. Although in the fans'
eyes the whole handsome gang shared the jokey
reputation of hellraisers, behind the scenes there
was only one, increasingly sad figure who was
actually becoming a professional burden. So when the
rescheduled tour of Europe began in June 2003, there
was only one question in the minds of the band and
the music press alike...

& give to the voice
in your heart♡

i wanna be...
i wanna be...
i wanna bleed your heart

I could buy the sweetest song suicide you all summer long (but that was only in
I wanna break your heart
(I made some here for you) your dreams)

& the pain I brought to you. Actually, I cannot
response many of these words is it popping or how to
describe that which it fits. Pop as fuck.   *chorus etc, many
my be sweetest melody   many meanings.

Art says (... out & when through a shock haze breach
her studio in (Shacklewell Lane) 'in a band, relationship
become... Beyond comfortable' everybody goes to
                                      their own rock
                                      healing?
                            Why ...   mistake
                            ...
                            No...

I met it and felt
& I thought
h...

I wont play live
my eyeless
me Uhont flowers/...ce on
all imaginary
soul from your
to not look
manner of illness

"WHERE THE HELL IS PETE?"

He'd not turned up at the airport and was apparently uncontactable.
The tension was understandable, given the impressive track record of
Mr Doherty in going AWOL when the band needed him. And as the minutes
ticked by on June 6th before The Libertines were due onstage at a
festival in Nuremberg, the band had a key decision to make. Cancel?
Perform as a three piece again? Or send out a message that he wasn't
irreplaceable, whatever the fans might think?

The compromise was to bring in their guitar tech Nick. Like any good
tech he knew his way round a guitar, and had got to know the songs. On
this first date too, The Cooper Temple Clause's Didz helped out on the
vocals, but as the tour limped on and Pete still hadn't got in touch,
Nick the guitar tech became Nick the official stand-in, playing
subsequent dates in Germany, Holland, Spain and France. The band were
nonetheless careful not to release Nick's surname - thus his role in
the band remained officially informal. It was a subtle point, but
already Doherty's bandmates were realising they were in a PR war.

Back in England, Pete Doherty had realised it too. When he resurfaced
it was to unleash a counter-attack at his friends with both barrels.
His rambling tirade on the band's official website attempted to
suggest that Carl, not Pete,
was the unreliable one.
He also implied that he was
the only one who cared about
the fans.

'Carlos did not show last night, as you know,' began Pete, in reference to
one of the band's many 'secret' gigs. These had been an article of faith in
the early days, shows aimed specifically at the inner circle of fans and
friends, often held 'at home' in The Albion Rooms. 'For me... this is
signal enough,' he continued, with a classic addict's self-justification.
'I will not be in Brewery Rd at 4.00pm today for the tourbus. I will not
vent my rage and wonder and hope and Arcadian sublimities alongside Mr
Barat for now. How can I... he had promised to come.'

Amidst the justification came a confused moment of weakness, an appeal to
the fans to be his friend and to take his side, which prompted a flood of
supportive postings. 'I'm so warped by having to play alone again that
you'd not cherish my company,' he sighed, inviting the chorus 'No, Pete,
we'd always need you here…' Sure enough, the comfy blanket of fan-worship
closed around him, but the only sense in which Pete had to play alone was
in his own mind.

Doherty had suggested he was in Leicester 'on a path of healing',
although quite why anyone would want to go to Leicester except to score
was quite another matter. A clearly exasperated Libertines spokesperson -
their then manager Banny Poostchi - did not even try to defend his
actions in PR-speak. Asked why Pete felt the way he did, she sighed: 'I
have no idea. I can't speak for him. They're not splitting up, they're
not stopping playing music. They're not doing anything which isn't about
being a Libertine.' However, she was rapidly learning that with this
band, the usual platitudes didn't apply. As a final thought, she added:

> 'IT'S IMPORTANT TO GET ACROSS THAT NORMAL RULES DO NOT APPLY TO THE
> LIBERTINES.'

Well, a 'libertine' is defined as someone unrestrained by convention… or,
for that matter, morality.

The war of words continued throughout June as the band returned from Europe
to play their largest UK tour to date. Doherty continued to rail and rant
through the fans' website, although once more his complaints were tinged
with sadness and a painfully obvious need for emotional support. He wrote:
'Having spoken to Carlos it is true - he does not want to play with me, in
my current "condition"… I'm not sure what he means but he's deadly serious
and it's settled. It's clear.'

'There is no use moaning about it,' he moaned. 'It's the way it is. I'm
getting on with things without any of them, though god knows I love him.
It's not happening anymore and it's the way it is.'

He signed off with a barely ambiguous: 'Fuck 'em.'

Just months before, when he spat those same two words on 'I Get Along',
Libertines fans took it to mean 'Us against the world'. Now, as he curried
for public sympathy against his mates, Pete Doherty seemed intent on
turning the world against The Libertines. Before too long it would seem
like the world was against him, and he would need his band more than ever.

Meanwhile the rest of the group had realised that there was no point
speaking through interpreters if they wanted to seem in touch with the
fans. This time they put together their own response, choosing NME.com as
their public forum. However, the joint statement only served to confirm
what the fans already feared: Pete would NOT be featuring on the UK tour,
however many reassurances were made about his and the band's future.

'The Libertines are not splitting up and their future is secure. The Libertines will be going ahead with their UK tour even though Peter Doherty will not appear at the shows.'

'Peter is unwell and the band are very concerned for his well being, they have told him out of concern for his health that he needs to get better before he can rejoin them. They also want it to be known they fully support him through this difficult time.'

The statement went on to stress what an 'extremely difficult decision' it had been for his friends, but they vowed to continue 'so as not to disappoint their fans.' Instead of a gang of four waging war on the world, the story of The Libertines had descended into a PR war amongst themselves. The band begged for understanding, and many fans turned up determined to enjoy the gigs just the same.

Others came along just to chant 'Where's Pete?' over and over at the stage. Not much fun for stand-in Nick, who should have been revelling in the experience of a lifetime. Instead, he was the unwilling length of rope in a fans' tug-of-war, fielding V-signs and thumbs-up, being alternately insulted and patronised.

The rebel chants were audible from the very first night: June 20th at Manchester Academy, where Carl attempted to assuage the doubters by dedicating live staple 'The Delaney' to his troubled friend. But the biggest cheer of the night was reserved for new tune 'Don't Look Back Into The Sun' - penned, inevitably, by Doherty.

THE WRITING WAS ON THE WALL: try as Carl, John and Gary had to make The Libertines bigger than just Pete Doherty, it was obvious for the future success of the group that they simply had to get their most wayward talent back on board.

Intended as the band's next single, 'Don't Look Back Into The Sun' had already been recorded prior to the tour, with Doherty still on board. It was to be the last session with Bernard Butler. This appears to be much against the wishes of Butler himself - months later he was still insisting on his own website that he would be doing the second album, and was just waiting on a call from Carl to start work.

A cynic might suggest he was under no such illusion, but was happy to keep his name in the papers ahead of launching new project The Tears (people were learning fast that the name of The Libertines was a way to guarantee column inches). In any event such hopes as he did have would be scuppered when Doherty was brought back on board.

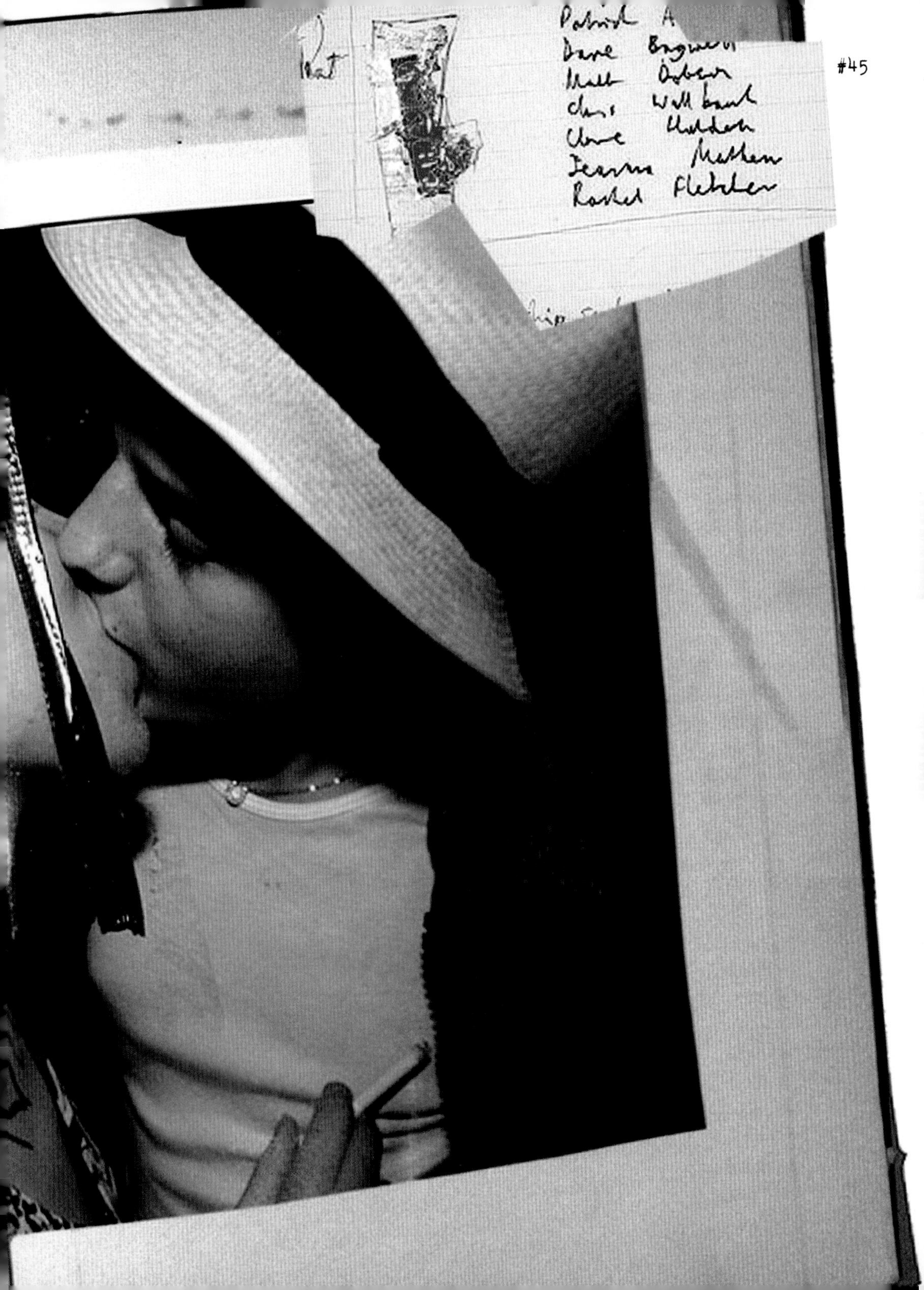
Patrick
Dave
Matt Dobson
Chris Wallbank
Rachel Fletcher

Pete had been Butler's main apologist when they first met, the only
one who remembered Suede with any fondness, but was subsequently
alienated by both his working methods and the final mix of their
debut single. Given their already stormy relationship (actually coming
to blows in the studio), the only surprise was that the former
Britpop idol was still in the picture as producer by the time this
session came along. It seems to have been a deliberate attempt to
reintroduce an air of discipline after the relaxed regime of Mick
Jones. But band photographer and friend Roger Sargent may have been
on the money when he said, 'The thing about Bernard is he's quite a
good taskmaster, but Pete doesn't take any form of authority very
well.'

Doherty himself was more graphic. 'All I can say, honestly and with
any clarity, is that Mick Jones is a libertine and Bernard Butler
isn't,' he told friend Pete Welsh.

'HE MAKES ME WANT TO HIDE IN THE CUPBOARD AND SMOKE CRACK.'

It's no coincidence that neither of the Butler singles ended up on
albums, although B-side 'I Get Along' did make it onto Up The
Bracket. In fairness to the man, however, this was a judgement made
less on merit and more on feel - retrospectively even Pete agrees
that the Butler sessions produced some of their most enduring cuts.
What's more, Butler had won the sympathy of the rest of the band for
the way he tried to deal with Pete. The best explanation for why
these singles didn't fit on the albums is aesthetic rather than
political: The Libertines' work with the former Suede man has a
slightly different flavour to the roughshod beauty they captured with
Mick Jones, who was happier just to let the boys plug in and play.
Besides, great bands had always thrown out classic non-album singles,
from The Beatles to The Stone Roses and Oasis.

But if the choice of producer was an
attempt to rein in the prodigal son, it
was a botch job. Mick Jones may have been
more tolerant of late starts and drunken
takes - but then he understood how the
band worked. After a session characterized
by no-shows and thrown punches, 'Don't
Look Back Into The Sun' had to be pieced
together from Pete's guide vocal takes and
Butler's own guitar overdubs. By sheer
good luck (and some very good raw
material) the track still sounded
releasable, but the experiment in
controlling Doherty had failed.

A press statement to announce the new
single gave Carl a platform to appeal to
his co-writer's better nature - or at
least, attempt to flatter him back into
the picture. 'We're very close. We're
brothers,' he insisted at the launch.
'Some strong forces took him away. He's a
dear friend. And he's such a good singer.
I miss my friend, god speed him back.'

Sadly events were about to take over the
band in a way that would mean they never
had control of their lives again. Carl's
'friend' was about to do something that
would attract the attention not only of
Her Majesty's Police, but also (far more
invidiously) that of the tabloid press.

pink
pandemonium
promotions

Pete D...

Babys...

Exiled 'LIBERTINE' Fro...
to play TWO special s...

Solo show @ ...

In the build-up to the notorious July 2003 break-in, it's worth considering how Pete had been occupying himself while the band were on tour without him. Drugs, obviously, took the main part. He had made a bunch of new 'friends' since Carl moved out, including the proprietor of a notorious Camden crack den. He'd done a couple of days in rehab and ducked out. He'd shaved his head and lost a worrying amount of weight. He had witnessed the birth of his first child with then-girlfriend Lisa Moorish. And he'd rowed and split with her too.

Not forgetting that all the time he'd carried on writing and performing music. He was still proprietorial about the name of The Libertines, and during his exile had tried to hijack the name to perform under himself. With a couple of Yorkshiremen on board, he even joked they should be called t'Libertines. But eventually, after numerous problems getting booked by confused promoters, he realised that if he wanted to strike out on his own, he needed his own identity. (There was of course the legal issue to consider, but then such factors never did bother Peter Doherty).

Me & my son

Hence **BABYSHAMBLES** were born. In his anaesthetic haze and neurotic need for recognition, the birth of this 'baby' was plainly of more emotional importance to Pete than that of his own child. He'd duly turned up at the July birth, according to the mother, but 'that was what it was' and no more. His new band, on the other hand, were a fresh start, a chance to vindicate himself.

Unfortunately, his fanatical followers and fawning supporters at
the NME in this case did him no favours. Babyshambles were
exactly as advertised: a sham, a shambles, at best an infant.
Pete was always gifted at those little Finnegans Wake-esque
pieces of wordplay, more so really than at playing guitar; and
be it subconscious or not, the name he gave this project
perfectly encapsulated the sad truth. Where The Libertines as a
brand label was in the 5-star brandy league, 'Babysham' was an
alcopop.

With former Libertine 'Scarborough' Steve on board, all the old
Camden hangers-on hoped to recognise something of those glorious
early days about the new band, and were willing to ignore the
ropey performances in the push to be part of the traditional
stage invasions. If they'd listened closely, they might have
noticed that their lyrical Pied Piper was just drunkenly
shouting out the names of the mid-nineties QPR football squad
over a haze of feedback.

Retrospectively it is hard not to see the Babyshambles story as
signalling the beginning of the end for The Libertines, but
there was a long road ahead before the fate of Doherty was
separated from that of his first band. He saw his fledgling
project as the embodiment of some new-found ability to stand up
to 'big brother' Carl; it was also the only way he could keep
playing and performing music 24-7. Even when he had The
Libertines he would still complain he wanted to be playing more,
bemoaning the nine-to-five hours in the studio, wishing he could
stay up cutting tracks all night - so in that sense he might
have needed the side-project whether he was welcome in Carl's
band or not.

However, it would be wrong to sell this second-rate pub-band experiment as a healthy distraction; at least, not at a time when the rest of his life was hitting new lows. It didn't keep him out of trouble, it didn't see him at his best musically or stretching himself in any way. It only helped to foster resentment and rivalry towards his old band, who were still doing their best to keep the door open for him.

ON JULY 25TH 2003,
THOUSANDS OF MILES AWAY,
THE LIBERTINES WERE PUSHING ON IN
DENIAL.

More specifically, they were in Japan; but that didn't stop Pete Doherty from crashing back into their lives. You could say he re-entered the band's consciousness through the back door - or rather the inadequately-hinged basement door. Needing money for drugs and still full of rage at his ex-best mate, he raided the home of Carl Barat and in the process took the onus of dealing with him away from his immediate circle and passed it on to the old bill. All things considered, it was not Pete's finest hour.

Doherty was arrested on a tip-off, and taken to Horseferry Magistrates Court in central London. To this day he resents the mother of his child, Lisa Moorish, for shopping him - but however distanced he was from reality, he can't have expected to get away with it. Not when he immediately told friends of Carl what he'd done, and when he'd even been rumbled casing the joint at another friend's flat earlier that night.

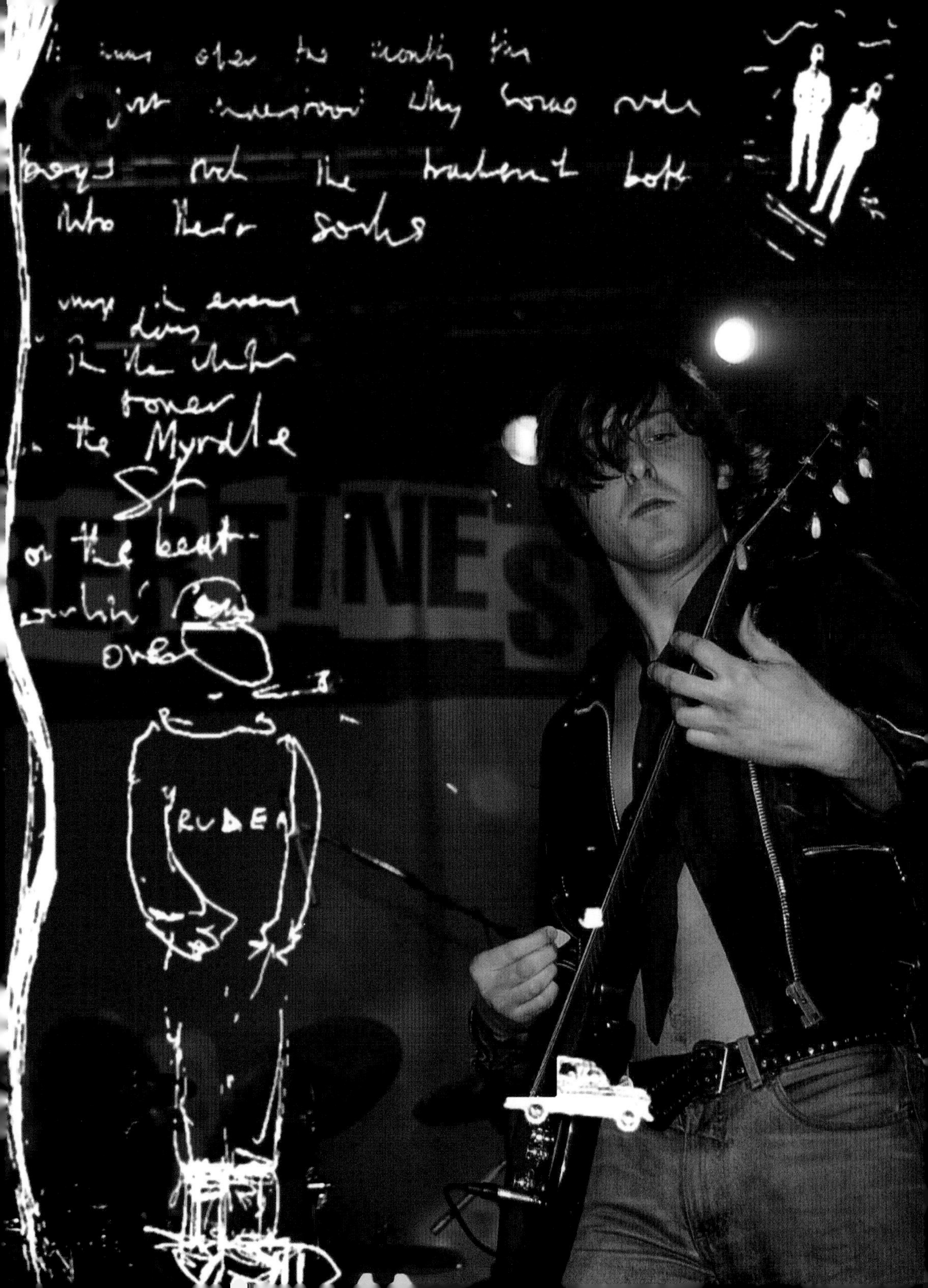

into their socks
the Myrtle
St
on the beat
RUDE

It's hard to see where the defence lies - effectively, Doherty was permanently in a state of diminished responsibility during this period, but testing positive for Class A drugs has never made a policeman look more kindly on a burglar. Still, he was keen to portray himself as some kind of Robin Hood figure, insisting that despite the drugs in his system, the money was for people worse off than him. 'I went to speak to Carlos about how I had a drummer and bass player living on my floor. They are on the dole and I needed to pay them because they are musicians. I was going down to Carlos's to say I can't pay them out of my own money,' he offered.

There is plenty of evidence of Carl and Pete's generosity in the past. Both remember the other giving large sums of money to the homeless in unmarked envelopes soon after receiving their first advance (a trick previously pulled by The Stone Roses' Ian Brown among others). Pete tells a story of Carl on Brick Lane handing this faded Northern beauty a grand and a half and nobody quite knowing how to react, her just shouting at him in confusion down the street. Pete himself claims to have given away 800 notes to a tramp on the Charing Cross Road.

He also announced on signing the deal and getting his own place that he could pay back "'anyone whose sofa I'd ever kipped on, who I'd ever scrounged a spliff off.' It's true there was a sense of community, of shared success and resources, and of no-one quite realising the value of money - certainly when they were all living at The Albion Rooms together. But when Pete kicked Carl's own door down, he knew he was transgressing. 'I've done something really bad,' were his words to Lisa; not out of remorse, it should be emphasised, but out of fear. He may have thought Carl owed him, but much as he may have hated the word 'junkie', this was junkie logic in action.

Doherty recalls shadow-boxing with himself outside Carl's
flat before he crossed the Rubicon. He claims he thought
he was arguing with Carl when in fact he was shouting at
his own reflection. 'When I realised, I booted the door
in. I was engulfed by complete misery and despair,' he
sighed. 'It was, "Why are you ignoring me?" - a cry from
the darkness.' The 'cry for help' aspect of his actions
cannot be ignored, but it must be tempered with the
knowledge that his behaviour was no different to that of
thousands of addicts in a cycle of crime.

THE PRESSURES OF FAME, THE NEED TO BE
CREATIVE, THE DESIRE FOR A STAGE, THE
SENSE OF INJUSTICE - THESE MOTIVATIONS
SEEM MORE GLAMOROUS BUT ARE ALL
ULTIMATELY SUBORDINATE TO THE CHEMICAL
NEED.

This made it all the sadder to hear him tell the papers:
'You don't go to rehab, you just kick it. It's got to
come from within.' He was claiming debts of £300,000 but
apparently wouldn't accept his record company's offer to
go on a course (he had dabbled with rehab earlier in the
summer but left after a few days). Such empty words made
his grovelling seem equally false. 'It wasn't revenge. I
do feel remorse, I feel sick,' he told the **Standard**, but
this is in total contrast even to the accounts of his
friends at the time.

He was still ploughing the same angle with Carl, claiming he just
wanted to work harder creatively than his bandmate. 'Carlos is
happy to record an album, promote it for a certain amount of
time. I can't do that, I need to write songs.'

Yet out of this dismal low point fluttered unexpected hope. It
got the band talking, that was for sure. It got the whole country
talking, and that was something too. It also meant nobody could
deny Pete's problem any more, not even Pete. Everyone wanted to
salvage something out of the situation. The record company had an
investment to protect, and immediately talked up the prospect of
a reunion once Doherty was out of prison. They could fulfill
their social obligation with talk of care and rehabilitation,
while scarcely unaware that their product was becoming bigger
than ever.

This should not be read as a swipe at corporate cynicism - there
is no doubt that Rough Trade care for their roster. In a dirty
industry, Geoff Travis has a reputation for putting his artists'
interests first, while A&R man James Endeacott had a personal
relationship with the band that went way beyond professional
courtesy. He is on record as saying 'We just wanted Pete to be
better - Rough Trade didn't care if the band never made another
record again.'

But for a band that everybody was so justly excited about, there
had been genuine disappointment about the first album sales - and
if they were going to relaunch a career, it was going to be on
the back of notoriety. That was something they couldn't change
even if they'd wanted to.

Pete for his part suggested he might yet join the band for appearances at Reading and Leeds, beginning some process of redemption for the shambolic displays the previous summer. Carl was more circumspect, and a statement was released saying they would definitely fulfill the dates without him; however privately he was paving the way to a possible reunion. He was prepared to play the big man for now, but all eyes would be on that particular relationship from this point on.

Sure enough, 'Don't Look Back Into The Sun' was released on August 18th and became their biggest hit to date, reaching #11 in the UK Chart.

This cannot be put down solely to the publicity factor. Put simply it's a brilliant song, and The Libertines' chart positions had steadily increased with each release: Top 40, Top 30, Top 20 and now just outside the Top 10. This is of course a desirable but natural progression for any breaking band,

and not out of the ordinary; but we must remember that nearly all the publicity the band had received since 'A Time For Heroes' made #20 had been negative. Bad shows, no-shows and robbery had defined their 2003, while slow sales continued to dog their first album. Sure, their next move had been awaited with much curiosity and 'Don't Look Back Into The Sun' was embraced by radio very quickly, even before July 25th. Still, it must be acknowledged that the fuss with the law in the build-up to this release did the sales no harm at all.

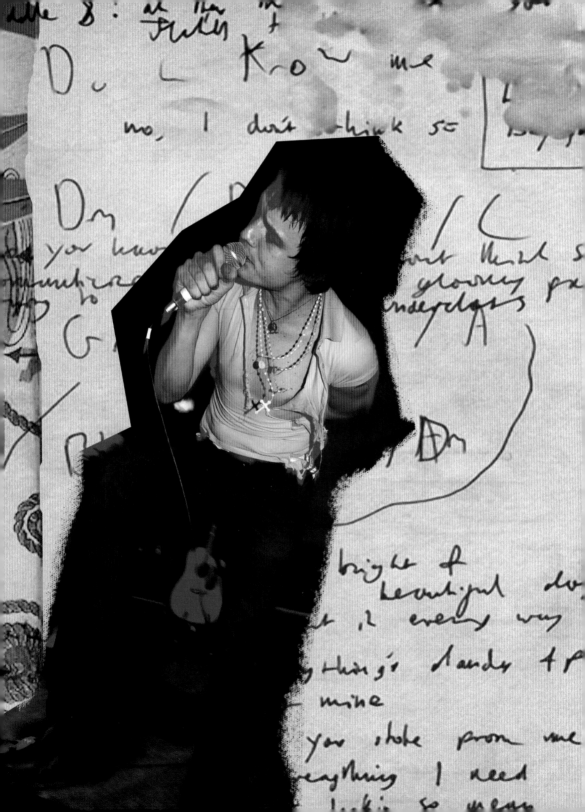

The band were not out of the woods yet, however. With
Doherty's sentencing due in September, the situation
would get darker before it got just gloomy.
Doherty's lawyer Richard Locke was hoping that evidence
of his drug addiction would lead to a community sentence
around which he could structure a treatment programme. It
was a reasonable plea, but the task of defending Doherty
was a thankless one. The judge immediately took against
the young punk, as quick to begrudge his looks and his
wealth as any jealous journo or Camden scenester: 'He
probably was suddenly earning too much money for his age
and began behaving irresponsibly. Unlike most of us who
have to study and work hard, they suddenly acquire
wealth.'

On one level, what His Honour said was true - at least in
the first part. But Doherty did not help his cause by
reacting badly to the second suggestion. As had happened
with Carl, he found himself being patronised by someone
in a position of power over him. 'I HAVE worked hard,' he
protested, with something between a whimper and a snarl.
Judge Roger Davies was unimpressed and issued a shock
custodial sentence of six months, adding that the serious
nature of the offence was compounded by his apparent
contempt for 'a colleague and a friend'.

There was a stunned reaction in the stands.

Friends gasped and family wept as the new dad was led
down to the cells. Locke immediately started to outline
the basis for appeal, stating in mitigation that this was
an 'impulsive act' carried out in a 'highly emotional and
drug-addled state'. Afterwards he briefed press on his
hopes to see the sentence reduced, but some time in
prison was now inevitable.

In desperation Locke had admitted to the court what he
felt the true motivation was behind the raid - and it
wasn't the drug money: 'There is a long and acrimonious
history between him and Mr Barat. Mr Doherty's perception
was that he had been victimised and betrayed by the rest
of the band.' It was not what the fans wanted to hear, but
fortunately it wasn't to stand in the way of a reunion -
at least, not officially. All the talk was about how Carl
would welcome Pete back into the fold the minute he was
out.

Sure enough the six months was duly reduced at Middlesex
Guildhall Crown Court, the sentence halved on appeal and a
further third taken off in respect of his 'guilty' plea.
So six months became two and two became one for 'good
behaviour' - surely the only time since his choirboy days
Peter Doherty had earned such an accolade. And true to his
word Carl was there for Pete when he walked on October 8th
- later that night they played together for the first time
in months, in front of 200 fans pinching themselves at the
Tap N' Tin club in Chatham, Kent. There were the
traditional stage invasions and even talk of a Christmas
single. First of all Pete and Carl needed time together,
first to confront their mutual demons, and second to write
the songs that would make up the new album. But Pete still
had other irons in the fire.

By this point Rough Trade had realised that the
Babyshambles bandwagon would probably rumble on,
and for safety's sake they had better embrace it
rather than risk alienating their contracted star.[10]
It became a legitimate side-project, a chance for
Pete to offload the stuff that Carl for whatever
reason didn't like (starting with the name itself).

'They're the most extreme band I've ever worked with,' said the former guru of Oasis and Primal Scream. 'It's sort of not rock 'n' roll. I don't know what it is - mental illness, probably.'[12]

Despite the imposing reputation McGee was a genuine fan. In the end it was good intentions and pastoral care that helped him guide the band as far as he could, which meant squeezing one more album out of the fragile central relationship. Although at the time it seemed she'd decided to settle for being a footnote in history, frankly Pootschi's achievement in lasting long enough to see 100,000 album sales begins with hindsight to look rather more impressive.

Both Pete and Carl had to make token gestures of sacrifice to get the band back together. Pete ditched Steve from his band, and The Libertines had to say 'ta very much' to replacement guitarist Anthony Rossomando, who'd helped them through their summer tour commitments. As the name suggests, he might as well have been imported from The Strokes. Friend and biographer Pete Welsh described him aptly thus: 'All skinny hair and New York chic, he looked like an amalgam of all five Strokes. But he wasn't Pete Doherty.'

He might have looked good on stage, hit fewer bum notes and kept his trap shut, but there was no way Anthony Rossomando and The Libertines were going to enrapture the fans like the Pete 'n' Carl show. It was never suggested he was doing anything more than keeping someone else's place warm, so Anthony and the boys parted on good terms. It was just as well, it probably occurred to all of them he might yet be needed again.

CHILDREN LITTLE GIRLS
BOYS WITH MOTHERS
I NO LONGER CARE
CARE. I AM.
FOR ME. PAY
DOWN. RUN YOURSELF A BATH.
IN YOURSELF. YOU. YOU YOU
ALL THAT
SHALLOW ICONS
CHRONIC
FUCK ME FROM

The band closed out an impossibly difficult year
in celebratory fashion, with a riotous December
mini-tour and the original line-up. Three nights
at the Kentish Town Forum demonstrated what the
fans had been missing, with Pete bringing his own
kind of chaos back to proceedings on the closing
night. Despite security arrangements designed to
prevent stage invasions, he announced that the
band couldn't possibly play the last number
'without at least another 65 people', who all
promptly obliged. This followed an eccentric
dream-come-true on the first night, when Pete
accompanied childhood heroes Chas 'n' Dave onstage.
While Parklife-era Blur had once attracted mocking
comparisons for aping their barrow-boy stylings,
with Doherty's open endorsement The Libertines had
done the impossible - and made Chas 'n' Dave cool.
Well, for about ten minutes at least.

2004 began well for The Libertines - February
saw them named Best British Band at the NME
Awards. But anyone looking for happy omens
should remember they began their annus
horribilis 2003 in exactly the same way. As if
to emphasise that unqualified fan loyalty just
wasn't enough, they would even claim the title
again in 2005 - despite having essentially
ceased to exist as a band. In any event, Peter
Doherty would not be present at the awards
ceremony in Hammersmith Palais, setting a
pattern for his trademark disappearances,
which he would continue through the year.

His first public episode of the New Year came
in early March at Brixton Academy. When
Doherty flew off the handle without warning
and trashed his guitar mid-set, the rest of
the band followed him offstage - partly a show
of solidarity, partly morbid curiosity to see
what was wrong.

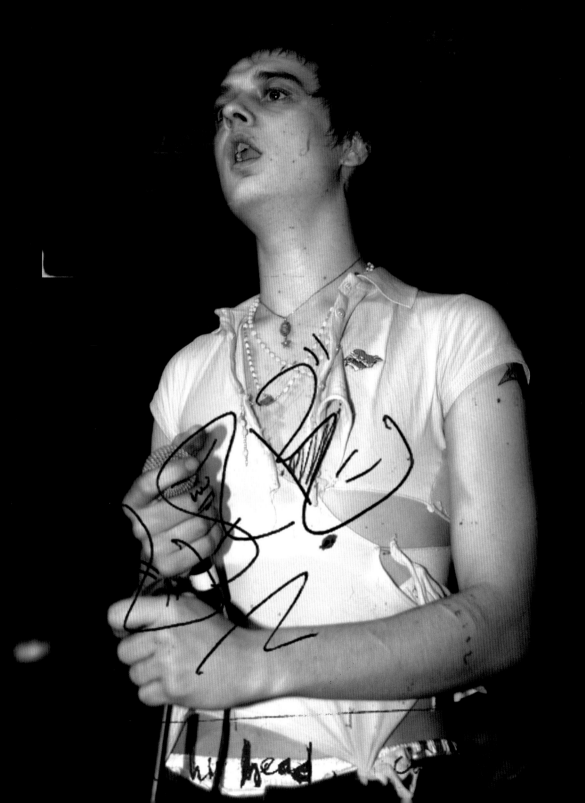

After a quick conference in the wings the band returned to the
stage as a three-piece, with bassist John Hassall on backing
vocals, and this time Pete was able to cool down quick enough to
slope back on stage before the end. 'Sorry about that. I had a bit
of a strop,' he offered as he joined the band for a rendition of
'Good Old Days'.

But any hopes that this might represent a coming to his senses were
premature - he'd cooled down by slashing his chest, a different kind
of self-harm to his usual and sadly not the last
time he would resort to it.

2004 would prove to be a strange year, both the
year when The Libertines truly made it big and
the year in which the story of Pete Doherty
would finally, unmistakably become separated
from theirs. The seeds were sown with the
announcement in February that he would be
releasing a spin-off project with his Camden
pal Wolfman. They'd often gigged together in
the smoke and chaos of the last three years,

but the Wolf was too much his own guy to subsume himself into some
vague Babyshambles concept. He had a song and he wanted Pete to
sing it.

Libertines fans weren't too worried, the February announcement
seemed to suggest that both Pete AND Carl would be doubling up on
the project. In a sense they weren't misled, but this wasn't a
collaborative effort to bond the old writing team. Carl's role was
very much restricted to the B-side, 'Back From The Dead', a
familiar rockier number on which he played guitar and sang. This
may have been a political move from Wolfman, trying very much to be
a mutual friend - as everyone on the scene tried to be. However,
the name on the CD cover was clear and unambiguous: 'Wolfman feat.
Peter Doherty, For Lovers.'

What's more, the A-side was far and away the memorable half of the project. An
extraordinary departure for Doherty, here was what the papers like to call a
'soaring ballad' - the warm MOR production and sense of lushness disguised the
very limited, very simple and somehow very beautiful song. A surprise and even
a let-down to some fans, nevertheless most Doherty devotees (who would have
found the style total anathema in the hands of, say, Elton John) were able to
let go and allow themselves to love it. The song made the UK Top Ten that
April, tellingly something no other Libertine had yet achieved. While the song
was plainly commercial much of the credit must go to the Doherty factor: both
the poignancy he lent the lyric that lifted it out of blandness, and the more
tiresome fact that everything he did now was now news. Post-prison, the 'Pikey
Pete' tabloid character had been born, even if this song was very much the
work of his other persona: Pete, the People's Poet. Both, however, were catchy
enough to sell newspapers.

Although work was well underway on the second, self-
titled Libertines album - again
with Mick Jones at the helm - the
solo momentum was continued when
Doherty's next release was
announced under the Babyshambles
moniker.

The 2,000-copy limited-edition
single was to be released by a
London indie label called High
Society, with the blessing of Rough
Trade, who still had a contractual
stake in all Doherty's output but
wanted to see where this one was
heading. The song itself, eponymously
titled 'Babyshambles', had been the
set opener at one of the notorious
early gigs where Pete tried to use
the 'Libertines' brandname. The
promoter had simply cherrypicked the
first title on their setlist and
advertised the band as that instead.

It was also one of the tracks Pete had tried to foist on Carl during a recording session in America, but he'd responded very negatively - not least because Pete had chosen fill the NY studio with his crackhead buddies. 'I wasn't having it. I didn't like the name, I thought that bore no relevance to anything, apart from Pete's shambles,' he spat later. One way or another, Pete got the tracks down and labelled them the Babyshambles Session, and the seeds of independence were sown.

The 2004 version, featuring two newcomers Patrick and Seb on bass and drums, didn't seem to be offering any great threat to The Libertines empire: according to bandmates, Carl Barat was more worried about the rise and rise of new critical darlings Franz Ferdinand. So he gamely went along with the Babyshambles launch party, an occasion that seemed to fans to be right back in the spirit of the old Libertines. 'What a night, what a cracking night! Stage invasions, club got wrecked, gig was stopped, ended up having a street party with Pete on guitar... Total rock and roll!' one excitable fan posted on NME.com.

Sure enough, The Underground in Stoke-on-Trent truly got a pasting on that night of April 21st, but not before a Pete guest spot with support act The Paddingtons, an impromptu Libertines acoustic set with Pete and Carl reprising 'What A Waster', and finally a midnight Babyshambles show. Again reports of the latter focus more on the antics than the tunes, with Doherty tugging at the poorly-fixed club décor until the entire audience did likewise and caused the walls to collapse.

This only meant the party spilling out into the street, where the reunited frontmen led a crowd singalong from the tourbus which was only broken up by the police. It was the kind of carefree night The Libertines built their live reputation on, but in the more innocent spirit where the crowds were dispersed peacefully and the promoter was charmed rather than incensed. 'The evening ended in what can only be described as a rock and roll manner!' he guffawed like a geeky dad as he counted up his night's takings. Babyshambles were even invited back the next week, perhaps to go some way towards compensating for the several thousand pounds' worth of damage.

Sadly the wider exposure Babyshambles were actually getting as a live act would not do Pete's reputation any favours. In fact worried punters were writing into fanzines all through May speculating about his health. Maybe they wanted to believe he was ill to excuse the disappointment of his shows - but if they were right about one thing, he certainly was on the drugs with a vengeance. By the second Friday in May he had been admitted into The Priory.

His brief stint at Farm Place clinic the previous summer - actually, make that a very brief stint - was optimistically seen by record company and bandmates as an 'intervention', an abortive effort but the first admission that something might be wrong. Somehow in between 'Shambles gigs and Olympic benders, The Libertines had managed to finish the recording sessions for their second album before packing him off to hospital.

However it was clear in his missives from within the walls of the expensive London quack-den that he was in deep and feeling very isolated. 'I'm fine… they've whacked me on loads of medication,' he began reassuringly. 'Very deranged and murky recollection of the last few days. A gaggle of nurses around my crinkly bed, they all jump as I wake up and yelp something about jelly. Then I notice a needle sticking out of my arm and spots of blood. What the fuck is going on? Vomit and shrieks, some girl warbling down the corridor in a towel.'

These thoughts were being posted not on The Libertines website as before, but on the Babyshambles one - his own domain. 'At least my laptop is here still,' he sighed with pathos. 'The only one who ever stood by me.' A self-pitying joke perhaps, but the fact was that he felt utterly abandoned by Carl. He did receive one visit from his bandmate at The Priory, which was one up from prison, but claims dismissively not to remember anything about it. Before long he was putting it about that he was on suicide watch.

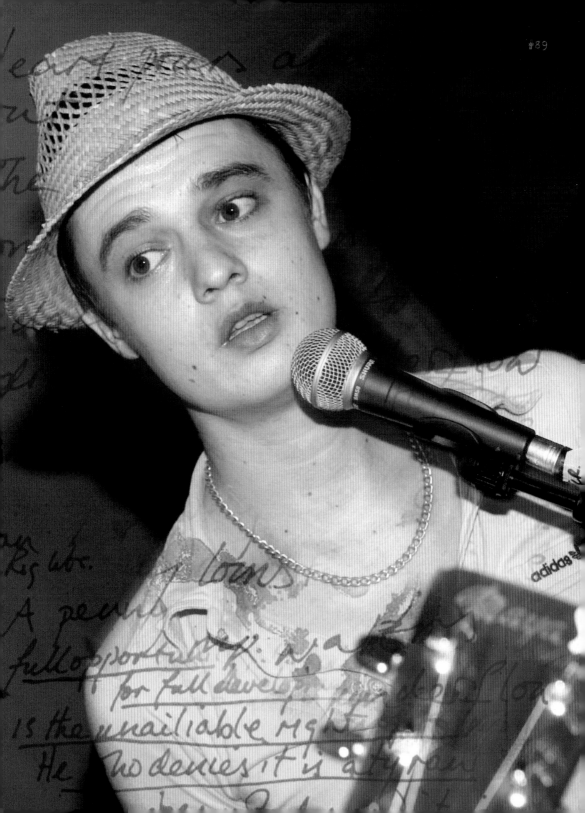

'Evidence of self-harm upon my skinny person but nothing could be
further from my mind as I awake brighter tailed and bushier eyed than I
have done for many a year,' he informed readers of babyshambles.com with
all the chirpiness of a man on 16 differently-coloured forms of
methadone. Coming across like Jack Nicholson protesting his own sanity
in **One Flew Over The Cuckoo's Nest**, he claimed the nurses kept checking
on him because they discovered old scars: 'Enough to make anyone give up
crack and smack.'

But he also promised he was reconnecting with 'Peter Doherty, whoever
the fuck that may be'.'

He checked himself out after two weeks, a considerable improvement on
his last effort. However, no-one was pretending that an expensive
fortnight's rest-cure with a never-ending supply of mood sweeties
represented a full recovery. Considering he had admitted a six-figure
debt to his record company when quitting rehab the previous year, the
mind boggles at how far his liabilities had run to by the end of this
session.

Suddenly, with a make-or-break album waiting to be released, Pete pulled
the trigger on The Libertines. No longer speaking to **NME**, and even being
elliptical to his own website, it emerged that his chosen medium for the
announcement was... **The Sun.** So why had he chosen the enemy? Well, two
reasons really: one, because he could; and, two, because they'd pay him
for the interview (providing he didn't spill the beans to anyone else,
even babyshambles.com).

The interview amounted to a rejection of family and friends and a
wholesale denial of Carl. 'It's got to the point where Carl and I don't
speak except on stage,' he complained (obviously forgetting through the
tabloid press). 'It breaks my heart. He treats me badly and every time I
come running back like a battered housewife.

'I feel like I'm seeking the ghost of a former friendship but Carl gave
up on me years ago. If he comes and grabs me by the hand, maybe we can
reclaim the empire together. But for now I'm out of the band.'

In answer to the hundreds of thousands of fans he was disappointing, he replied simply: 'Surely no one wants to see me trapped in this cage that is only making me miserable.'[13] It was a very dark time, in which nobody seemed quite sure where he was, but everyone had a theory. Someone claiming to be Doherty did briefly pop up on the Libertines' website, begging his own starstruck fans to lend him a couple of grand. But like the characters in his Wolfman collaboration, 'Lovers running away, just for today,' he and his girlfriend were in fact eloping to France to recover.

In practice the escape lasted not much longer than the song suggested. As soon as his mother got wind and put her foot down, he went scuttling back to rehab - first in France and then for a second shot at The Priory. Rumours were flying around the web about what had happened to him, with fears that he had already become the next Richey Manic, but Alan McGee tried to appeal for calm. 'He is truly in really good medical hands so please stop the rumours,' he begged. 'His mum is constantly with him at present and she has been brilliant.' Not so very rock and roll anymore, but definitely the fallen angel who had the fansites overflowing with offers to take care of him.

Before long, however, he had skipped the clinic and snuck out under radar once more. On the 7th June a concerned Libertines spokesman ditched the tactic of trying to keep a lid on the rumours in favour of a genuine plea for information: 'Peter left The Priory this morning, his whereabouts are currently unknown although every effort is being made to find him. We are all very concerned for his well being.' Despite Pete's claim to have quit the band, the management was still insisting The Libertines were very much together and just waiting on their talisman's recovery.

Then suddenly he reappeared, that very evening, and it was onstage with The Libertines. The band hijacked the stage from headliners The Boxer Rebellion at the 100-capacity Infinity Club, the launch of the Libertines-endorsed Dirty Pretty Things night, and launched into a set of old classics plus forthcoming single 'Can't Stand Me Now'. On the night after Carl's 26th birthday, with a rousing closer of 'Good Old Days' and the promise of a new record to come, suddenly it must have seemed too good to be true. The NME proudly announced that they were 'far from splitting up' and even the news that Pete was about to jet off to Thailand for an intense course of rehab was heralded as unambiguously good news.

'If he's going to get clean permanently anywhere it's in this place,'
trumpeted Alan McGee. 'To be honest his mum, Carlos and myself can't believe
he did it but he's a man of many surprises.' He wasn't joking. The
Thamkrabok Monastery was a complete wild-card, and had been touted the
previous month by the tabloids after June Brown - **Eastenders**' Dot Cotton -
had recommended it to Pete. Of course the red-tops loved the 'odd couple'
angle, ignoring June's serious work promoting a drug charity in favour of a
comedy article. 'I'm a huge Libertines fan,' the 77-year-old, whose godson
had fought crack addiction, was reported as saying. It was all just one more
step beyond in the increasingly surreal life of Pete Doherty.

One day he's reported missing, then he's onstage with the biggest band in
Britain, and the next day he's being disciplined by manic monks in Thailand.

Sadly the Thai sticks proved to have more substance than the surreal dream.
Pete was not one of 100,000 souls who found sanctity in this ancient
spiritualism, and within three days of taking a religious vow never to take
drugs again was on a flight home as high as a kite. It is truly depressing to
re-read the snippets of genuine optimism from the day before he left, both
from him and those close to him. Pete had written the day after the gig: 'I
saw Mick Jones, Carl, John and Gary last night and I know I can mangle out
all the creases and live out further my grandly Arcadian dreams and dear
divine adventures all Albion's sons and daughters. I have some strength god
knows from wherein me. I want to live.'

Alan McGee had said to the public, to the press and the fans: 'All we ask of
you people is keep the faith in Peter Doherty and The Libertines. The man may
be away for a month, he may even reject the West and not return. In any event
the man we sent out there will come back a different man.' It must have been
genuinely deflating, even personally embarrassing to everyone involved to
explain that he was coming home on the next flight. Or rather, he wasn't -
he'd actually slipped off in the direction of party city Bangkok. The
Libertines had cancelled their summer festival dates so he could get well, and
he'd gone halfway around the world to find an opium den.

Of course, the tabloids were most interested in getting the quote from
Dot Cotton.

Things didn't get much better on his return. In fact, he was back in police custody within 24 hours of touching down - this time being charged with possessing an offensive weapon. He'd been pulled on a suspected driving offence and then searched on reputation, and they'd turned up a flick-knife. Whether this was bad luck or bad karma, it was certainly more proof that trouble stalked Pete Doherty mercilessly around the earth.

What's more, as the real story gradually emerged before the fans, he was now the only one left blaming his demons on others. That much was clear when he and Carl faced off in a famous August NME collectors' issue, with two editions for fans to choose - Carl's story or Pete's story. Carl was as eager as ever to offer the olive branch but sounded pessimistic about the future: 'I want to be in a band with my friend,' he protested for what must have felt like the zillionth time. 'That's all I can say to that. And that I don't think I want to be in a band called The Libertines if he's not in it, in the long term.'

Perhaps that could be perceived as a dig at Pete's prior attempts to co-opt the band name; perhaps he'd just had enough. From how Doherty describes the deterioration of their relation-ship over as long as three years, and even the stormy and competitive start, it was beginning to wear a little thin to hear Barat describe the prodigal son as his 'friend'. The way his bandmate describes it, the idea of some halcyon wonderland where they took on the world as best buddies, unbeaten brothers, seems as unreal and fantastic as Doherty's own searched-for Arcadia.

Pete for his part conceded that Carl 'needed his space'. But mainly he was back on the trail of self-justification. He took the opportunity to slam tabloid speculation that his drug habit was costing him £1,000 a day (a figure they still trot out to this day). 'I've never spent £1,000 a day on heroin, you'll die,' he stated baldly.

And rumours of his death were definitely premature.

Further ostracising people of late is the dear dreary Tabloids.
Bapples has sold her soul for tuppence and to my slow
dismay speaks slanderous witless nonsense to the
My depression has dragged ...

... only ... makes me single out individuals
for fucking up my head & breaking my heart. How
foolish I shall appear next page! Gas mark 5

Supermodel Kate had managed to ride out being tagged 'the face of the 90s' to become, if anything, even more chic in the 21st Century. Still topping all the best-dressed lists, she had graduated from waifish doll to boho rock-chick, an icon to slavish younger starlets like Sienna Miller. She had a child by trendsetting magazine editor Jefferson Hack but the union had crumbled over her wild-child antics.

Not only was she throwing increasingly debauched parties at home in Gloucestershire, where even the likes of Sadie Frost failed to keep the pace, but she was being constantly linked to rock'n'rollers. Friends with Oasis from her Johnny Depp days, she had become close to narcotic legend Bobby Gillespie of Primal Scream, even jeopardising his career by warbling on one of his records[16] - this along with numerous promo video appearances, most notably as a horny poledancer (doubtless inspired by Cher's ride on the banisters) in the White Stripes 'I Just Don't Know What To Do With Myself'. Given Kate's singularly onanistic performance, the song title was truly ironic.

She may have shared a name (and a sometime hard drug habit) with Katie 'Bapples' Lewis, the subject of 'What Katie Did', but perhaps the Doherty 'ex' with whom Kate Moss had most in common was fellow single mother Lisa Moorish.[17] With a child by Liam Gallagher as well as Pete Doherty, Lisa shared the same fatal attraction to irresponsible rockers - the only difference was, with her eight-figure fortune Kate was less likely to be chasing the gentlemen concerned for maintenance payments. There's roughing it for glamour points and there's actually living the life.

Kate had an eye for dangerous guitarists. She'd received a degree of tabloid mocking as some kind of arch-groupie when both Kasabian's Serge Pizzorno and Franz Ferdinand's Alex Kapranos knocked her back at Glasto for coming on too strong - the 'new Patsy Kensit', that was the slur. So it was pretty inevitable that Peter Doherty ended up on her guestlist for a little shindig in the Cotswolds, especially with the glam-rock theme.

Mick Jones' wife Miranda was one of Kate's inner circle - and Mick had been asked to share DJ duties, paving the way to an invite for his notorious protege. Miss Moss knew what she was doing. Her taste in bands was impeccable and deliberate, and she groomed her knowledge of London punk as carefully as her best pair of furry mukluks (that is, before they went into last-season storage). So despite the tabloid gasps it was no great surprise that the shambling North London smack victim should turn up at the Cotswold home of a supermodel. What probably WAS a surprise to 99% of the population was the fact that the two emerged from the other side of an all-nighter as some kind of item.

The signs were there the very next day when the planned lunch at Kate's local, The Swan in Southrop, was roundly snubbed by 35 hung-over and strung-out guests. Kate herself failed to emerge from her room, where she was boarded up with Doherty in a haze of skunk and a snowstorm of coke. This was not just a fling, we were led to understand. They were 'going steady'. Boyfriend and girlfriend. Soulmates, that was how Pete put it. 'It's been the best week in a long time because I've really found love,' he told the press almost immediately. 'I believe her when she says she loves me and I know I mean it when I say I love her.'

Mind you, almost all our understanding of the relationship comes from him; Moss remains one of the most guarded interviewees in the public eye today. It's partly because it keeps her intellectual mystique at a higher stock than many in her profession - better to keep quiet and be thought a fool than to open your mouth and remove all doubt. But also she keeps a frantically tight grip on her private image and insists on the discretion of her friends - and she needs to, given the flamboyance and decadence of her party lifestyle. Perhaps some clue to her own agenda was what Pete said about her when she dumped him the first time, before doing her obligatory stint in drug rehab. Doherty told **The Sun** that she hadn't left him because he wouldn't kick drugs but because 'I can't buy her diamonds and my dick is too small.' When he said it he probably wasn't joking.

You might think, therefore, that in allowing the disaster-magnet Doherty into her world she's made the worst decision of her life. Certainly her celebrity cohorts, from Sadie Frost to Jefferson Hack and even Bobby Gillespie, queued up to add their two cents, ranging from concern to outright disapproval. But if nothing else the girl understands sex, drugs and fashion, and Doherty ticks all the boxes. For some supermodels that pursuit leads them to Hollywood, to LA, the Oscars and, let's 'fess up here, The Betty Ford Center. To Pete's eternal gratitude, Kate's weakness is for rock'n'roll. She is impossibly glamorised by it - the way a rock'n'roller is glamorised by, well, a supermodel. If only the British press could be persuaded to see they were the perfect couple...

Certainly they were taking an interest. Which was just as well: 2004 had been as bad for Kate as 2003 was for Pete, in her own slightly more pampered way. The ubiquitous Sienna Miller had pinched her mate's husband as well as her look, and in some quarters was seen as pinching her crown (December's **Vogue** had named her 'Woman of the Year').

Meanwhile Kate's stock appeared to be falling for the first time. Named as a bad role model for both her smoking and her penchant for rabbit-fur - of course, when on-the-up Sienna did the same she was indulged as the next big thing - there were rumours in June that Chanel were going to drop Moss from a £1m contract. That was before the public humiliation of all that crashing and burning at Glastonbury, before taking on (shame of all shame) Victoria Beckham's cast-off as the face of Rocawear.

That year she had fallen out with both her friend Sadie Frost and the father of her child Jefferson Hack, who had moved out of their flat soon after her 30th birthday the previous year. The theme for that bash had been taken from F. Scott Fitzgerald's novel **The Beautiful and Damned**, and Kate told curious journos that she felt more damned than beautiful. But as **The Independent** said at the end of the year, 'NOT SO MUCH DAMNED, AS DOES ANYONE STILL GIVE A DAMN?'

Well, from January 2005 onwards, they definitely did. Tabloids, gossip mags, broadsheets, even **Private Eye** and the **Spectator** were running think-pieces on the odd couple. Pete Doherty was no longer a star without a product - his product was himself, his relationship, and his art was in wrecking everything he touched, running a public demolition derby.

To say that Pete Doherty's career was now in promoting his relationship would not just be a cynical stab, it is a literal truth. Even since the 'my drug hell' interviews the previous year, he had been earning his money doing deals with papers - the problem was, he had now given the same interview to just about everyone. Suddenly he had a new angle, talking about his true love, his 'saviour' - and there were pictures to sell as well.

One such person with whom he entered into a Faustian business pact was called Max Carlish. A fawning, starstruck fool who wanted to be accepted by Doherty even more than he wanted to be a film-maker, Carlish followed him around shooting and chatting until Doherty could take no more. Here was another abusive 'buddy' relationship, albeit skin-deep this time, and with Doherty now cast in the role of power. Carlish was tolerated because of the ego-trip, and because of a business relationship in which they agreed to share the profits of his snooping.

The first bitter fruits of this partnership were born on January 30th, when the **Sunday Mirror**, one of the many papers to have paid for a Doherty interview, ran a front-page 'exclusive' showing 'chilling photographs' taken by Carlish of the new Mr Moss apparently smoking heroin - or, as they put it, the 'pathetic fool chasing the dragon'. Finally Carlish was getting some reward now his idol had suddenly become so bankable - £30,000 worth, if the figures are to be believed, less of course his commission to Doherty. 'I told him he was welcome to some of the money for the film if he would use it for drug rehabilitation and get back into the studio,' whined Carlish piously. 'Then I thought: what if we could actually film him going into rehab? What a film we would have there!'

He doubled up by selling the same photos to the **News of the World**,
naturally, who appealed to Kate's better nature in one of their famous
'editorials': 'Look at this picture of your new lover smoking heroin,
and for God's sake, junk this junkie.' It was a lovely slice of moral
relativism from the newspaper who helped pay for his junk habit, but
assumed that their readers would buy the notion that because Kate was
beautiful, she was also pure.

Still, she was certainly furious that the pictures emerged - but not
because her eyes were finally opened to her lover's not-so-secret drug
habit, which seemed in any case to have been a feature of their
courtship. What it did wake her up to was the untrustworthy nature of
Doherty's entourage, and possibly even that of the man she barely knew
herself. In order to cover his tracks, desperate not to lose the woman
he kept telling the world he loved, Doherty did two things. One, he
denied everything. Two, he promptly went over and 'confronted' Max
Carlish - allegedly robbing him in the process, presumably for the money
he felt he was owed. Filmless, friendless and hard-up, Carlish cried
assault.

This landed Peter Doherty in the dock again, this time spending four
nights in Pentonville jail. Rough Trade hummed 'n' harred but eventually
found the considerable sum of £150k to help him make bail once again.
Still, rehab was another condition, and this time they weren't going to
pay. So how was the bill going to be met, considering Doherty's own
debts were already twice that? The same way he'd been meeting all his
bills, of course. He alighted straight from the clink to a meeting with
Sun reporter Sean Hamilton (just one of many journalists claiming to
'know him best'), where he gave yet another interview promising to 'stay
clean', if not for his own sake then for his angel Kate. At the bottom
of the piece came the disclaimer: 'Pete Doherty has received no fee for
this interview, but **The Sun** has paid a £12,000 rehab bill to help him
beat his addiction - and to highlight the perils of drugs to thousands
of young music fans.'

So everyone was gratified. Doherty fulfilled the criteria of his bail.
The Sun got its exclusive, and a chance to take the moral high ground -
after a year of evidently glamorising a soul in torment. Rough Trade,
for once, didn't have to foot the bill. In fact, everyone was happy
except for Kate Moss.

This trauma precipitated the first break-up, and thus a non-stop season of on-off, will-they-won't they, love-hate stories about Pete and Kate which recalled the glory days of The Libertines. Without Kate Moss uttering a word on the subject, somehow we knew about it every time she'd had enough, and then the papers feigned surprise every time they were then pictured together again. All this could fill a tabloid-sized page every day for a whole year, as it promptly did, but none of it was conducive to either of their productivity or mental health.

As for Carlish, the material he intended for a serious documentary was laughed out of the lobby at several production companies. However, seeing the potential in anything with the Doherty brand, Channel 4 managed to cobble together a programme called Stalking Pete Doherty: a comi-tragic look at the sorry life of the would-be Marti Scorsese himself, forever in hock to the man he was trying objectively to document. 'I realised just how smart he was,' he would gush. 'He rhymed green with spleen and even understood the medieval meaning of the word spleen.' Carlish tried to get onstage with Pete like some kind of fat brummie Bez, and unnerved viewers by relating the experience to a kind of 'mutual orgasm'.

Some cynics suggest Doherty's publicist and manager James Mullord even employed a real film crew to follow Carlish as he went about his own car-crash project. Either way, Carlish condemned his own credibility, and while we never really learned anything more about Peter Doherty, he was at least made to look good by comparison. All charges of assault were dropped in April 2005.

Around this time Babyshambles also managed to sneak out a Top Ten single, the lightweight but memorable 'Killamangiro'. A chorus stemming from that stream-of-consciousness wordplay that is Doherty's stock-in-trade, it boasted a delightfully low-life theme that seemed to recall the talent that got us interested in the first place.

Still, not everyone was impressed. Not Liam Gallagher, who despite offering Babyshambles a support slot publicly cast doubt on Doherty's responsibility towards his baby Astille - and complained He'd end up having to pay all the maintenance to Lisa Moorish. Nor ex-girlfriend Katie Bapples - furious when Pete presented a copy of the lyrics to 'her' song What Katie Did as a lovers' keepsake to his new 'Katie'. Not that he was proving much better at keeping hold of this one.

The first dumping was announced to the
world on Valentine's Day 2005, the
fledgling romance not yet a month old.
Moss was furious when for the first time
grainy photos of herself had ended up in
the hands of The Sun, taken from
Doherty's own phone.

He later claimed a friend had nicked his
mobile and gone behind his back - but
Britain's best-loved daily insist Doherty
met up with their man in rehab, even
showing off 'tender text messages' he had
exchanged with his lover. Hoping to stay
in bed with both **The Sun** and Kate Moss,
the desperately needy young man was
already lying to both his mistresses.

For his part Pete was upset Kate would
cause him pain at such a crucial stage
in his rehab programme, and over
something as petty as control of her
image. Perhaps it didn't occur to him how
important that was in her business.

Still, Kate had her own experience of
tabloid 'misrepresentations', so she was
more inclined than many to sympathise or
forgive. Most of her profession had some
axe to grind with the gutter press, from
Naomi Campbell to Sophie Anderton - in
fact since the latter's tearful (if well-
rewarded) tabloid confession to having
worked effectively as a prostitute, vile
rumours had flown round the city of a
£20k-a-night supermodel call girl
service. While Kate would have had no
need to stoop so low, it does seem a far
cry from the £20-a-go hand-jobs Pete
claims he was giving old queens in Camden
just four years before.[18]

les Effarés   #113

By the end of the month they'd been spotted together again after what the tabloids like to call a night of passion. 'I know people are saying he's no good for me, but I can't help myself,' ran a **Sunday Mirror** quote attributed to Moss. 'There's just something about him. I keep going back.' She was discovering what Pete Doherty's long-suffering fans and bandmates had felt for years.

Not all the press agreed with this interpretation of events, however. Others insisted throughout March they were still very much 'off', and cited a jealous confrontation in a Belsize Park boozer when Kate was out getting ratted with actor pal Rhys Ifans. Clearly not convinced he fitted in such exalted C-list company, Victoria Newton suggested in her Bizarre column that puppy-eyed Pete had started to follow her around like Max Carlish once stalked him. 'Please Kate, all I want to do is talk,' they'd have him say, while she screamed back 'Just go away, leave me alone, I've had enough.'

All this was satisfying the worst jealousies of frustrated husbands, teen bloggers and one-handed Page 3 'readers' alike, convinced that there was some cosmic injustice in this scruffy drug-user pulling one of the world's most beautiful women while they sat at home fantasising. Kate 'seeing sense' and dumping Pete every other week seemed to restore natural order to the universe - even if the truth was that of an ongoing, perpetually stormy relationship.

Suddenly April brought an almost comic change of gear, with talk of permanent splits immediately followed by whispers of marriage after Kate was seen sporting a gold band on her finger (in other words, 'Model wears jewellery shock'). By June it was 'official' with a joke ceremony at Glastonbury, where the notorious chapel of 'Love and Loathing in Lost Vagueness' provided an all-too-suitable venue for a staggeringly drunk one-day hippie nuptial ritual. Even potential love-rival Serge Pizzorno gave the match his blessing, snarling: 'That poor kid Pete Doherty is going to marry her. All I can say is good luck to him. He can have her. Because, otherwise, I think she'll be looking for a man for the rest of her life.' One day it was off because he'd been in a brawl outside a gig, the next it was back on because he'd been spotted buying some fancy underwear at a sex shop. The greatest talent in British music, the most important voice of a generation, had been reduced to a tawdry clown act.

Even worse, his was a mere sideshow. He was playing groom to a clothes-horse, and no-one was taking Babyshambles more seriously because of it. He was getting reviews in places which would never normally find room for live acts, like **Tatler** and **Bizarre** - and none of them could understand the concept of a gig where the act turned up late, you couldn't hear the words, and the sweaty drunks onstage were dressed like the sweaty drunks in the crowd. As a result, for all the column inches he was getting as pantomime villain, the only scattered mentions of his music all made the same 'Shambles' puns and mocked him for 'trying to be a rebel' (thank you for that insight, 3 am). Where mainstream publications did deign to give him a musical context, it was usually as 'ex-Libertines frontman' and not as his own act. Frustrated drummer Gemma Clarke had already seen this coming, quitting Babyshambles the very month Kate Moss came into their lives.

It was beginning to look like Doherty had thrown his hat in with the wrong crowd. Where Kate at first re-inspired him to a creative burst, by the summer she was already causing him to stagnate.

There was the gig in May supporting Oasis in Paris, the biggest in Babyshambles' confused history, that had to be blown out after Pete got into a jealous fit with Kate on the Eurostar. Then history repeated itself at Norway's Oya festival, where the band missed their prime slot after their singer endured an extended cavity search at Olso airport. The reason? Pete's 1.7g of coke and 1.5g of heroin, smuggled in to 'celebrate' the fact that he and Kate had just got back together for the fiftieth time. When he did finally get onstage he marked the occasion by vomiting on the somewhat diminished bunch of revellers in the mosh-pit.

But perhaps the summer's nadir was his performance at Live 8 with Elton John, who introduced him as 'a major new talent' but was later reduced to saying 'at least he looked good'. In fairness, Doherty's out-of-tune rendering of T-Rex's glam classic 'Children of the Revolution' was not the most embarrassing display of the afternoon - that honour goes to Madonna, striking up the band with Ethiopian famine survivor Birhan Weldu still stranded onstage and forced to do a little dance. But one fact that emerged afterwards was that EVERY act of the afternoon saw an increase in back-catalogue sales after the broadcast - except Doherty's. Babyshambles records were not even available, of course, but the two Libertines discs slipped further down the chart. The record TV audience meant a whole new section of the population had been introduced to a staggering drunk, singing off-key through a soggy fag with a national treasure forced into the indignity of backing him on piano. How could he make it any worse? Only by insulting Saint Bob himself, suggesting he only sang badly because his little girl Peaches Honeyblossom Geldof tried to come on to him just before he went on. Enough to give anyone a spasm of paedophilliac cringe, thankfully Doherty subsequently withdrew his latest excuse-cum-joke. Peaches may be above the age of consent, it is just that with a gormless quotient bordering on ESN consent would not be an admissible defence.

He was forced to apologise again at the end of July, this time to an 'innocent' **Mirror** journalist (their contradiction in terms, not mine). 24-year-old Laurie Hannah bought Doherty a drink but received a punch in the face once the guitarist had clocked who he worked for. 'What is it your paper calls me - fucking junkie scum?' he demanded of the dazed reporter. Clearly those Faustian pacts he had made with his most natural enemies were beginning to trouble him, not least because he perceived the press as influencing his relationship with Moss. The fact that he and his muse were on a downer at this point was clearly being taken out on this hapless guttersnipe.

So there were the live debacles and the self-hatred; then there was the waning muse. He had been in the studio recording the Babyshambles debut ever since being bailed in February, all through April and May as well, without getting any closer to a product. Songs were in such short supply that a revamped 'What Katie Did' - the 'Moss version' - had gone from private joke to serious album contender, despite the fact the original had been out less than a year.[19]

The album was taking so long that bookies were offering very long odds on whether it would be out for the advertised release date (pushed back to October 2005 and counting). Even worse, there was constant talk of a certain wannabe rock chick making an ill-advised vocal turn on the record; as Alan McGee had said (also in reference to Moss), 'Models on records do not work'.[20] Rough Trade was blithely insisting all was on target despite some fairly unimpressed rumours circulating about its quality and readiness.

Still, if you throw enough shit against the wall, you might get a hit - and come August Babyshambles did manage to squeeze out a second single proper. Despite failing to convert the uninitiated, 'Fuck Forever' followed in the spiritual footsteps of 'What A Waster' by dragging his heavily-censored potty-mouth back onto mainstream radio. With a summer of almost constant bad publicity behind him, Pete was in the Top Ten again. And to celebrate he was soon brawling, most usually with other musicians, often over Kate Moss.

His flighty lover was being linked in the press with members of The Bravery and Bodyrockers - Christ, from someone of her supposed taste that must have felt like a deliberate act of rudeness. That same month an attempted arson attempt in his own bedroom was seen as a cry for help. Pete was shipwrecking himself trying to please a model who had gone from beautiful muse to monkey on his back. And, if only the tabloid press would see it, she was the one holding HIM back when HE could do better.

It all backfired for Moss, as the world and his aunt was saying it would. On Thursday September 15th The Mirror ran with a world exclusive, 'COCAINE KATE'. One of Pete's entrepreneurial mates had secretly filmed an all-night studio session, in which Moss herself could be seen racking up line after line on her beautiful long legs. The grainy images prompted outrage but not surprise, not from editors nor her own parents, who joined in one voice to blame her shambling consort.

No-one could seriously have doubted that Kate Moss was fond of cocaine, nor even that it got her up in the mornings and helped her control her appetite. Certainly not the tabloid hacks who use it to stay up all night chasing deadlines; but they had their revenge on her for forcing them to settle out of court the last time they'd run a story about her Class A habit. All the tabs focused on Kate the liar and hypocrite, after THEY had portrayed her as the helpless victim in the relationship.

'I don't do any Class A's, especially not heroin,' she'd told Channel 4 (some seven years previously). 'I've seen what it does to people.' The following Sunday, the **News of the World** revealed that she'd had threesomes with various mates, females mainly... well, sometimes Jude Law.

As middle England mourned the loss of a pure and beautiful soul, Babyshambles' fans might have noted with dismay the real hard-luck story of the set-up: halfway through September, and the album still not ready for mixing. The pictures which most worried music lovers weren't those of a super-groupie doing lines of coke: they'd be the ones of her giggling at the desk with her rudderless artist gigolo, helping twist the knobs and joining in the creative process.

Babyshambles' fans would mourn the fact that an album they'd waited all year for, one they'd kill just to hear a single snippet of, was being used as a rack for a spoilt prima donna's £200-a-day charlie habit. 'I haven't heard it,' she admitted between lines of snorting the Bolivian marching powder. And as of Autumn 2005, neither has anyone else.

As for The Libertines, the history book is not yet fully written. A movie of their lives has been mooted, though in the immediate term a short film documenting a guerrilla gig at The Albion Rooms is attracting previews at the Sundance Festival.[21] Alan McGee, on record as calling them the most important band in the world today, has suggested that were the original line-up to be reunited, they would sell three million albums. But Pete had more important things on his mind - keeping Kate on his arm.

At first Kate brazened it out with him and they swanned around New York telling the slavering newshounds to eff off. However, not even love and charlie combined can stave off the claims of a £10-million-a-year modelling habit. The lawyers, agents, advisors, hirelings, sundry agony aunts and cancelled modelling contracts eventually made her see sense... well, where everyone's bread was buttered. She dumped Pete and retreated into rehab in Arizona.

Pete's curious position as London's most celebrated junkie meant he could pick and choose his shoulder to cry on. In this case, it was his favourite newsreader, the BBC's motherly Kirsty Wark, and the forum was once again Newsnight. 'I'll love her for ever,' he told the nation on December 23rd. 'But whilst I'm in any way connected to crack or heroin or if my life revolves in anyway around these drugs, then I can't be in her life.'

If he was belated trying to protect Moss's career, he was doing a good job (though he notably left cocaine out of that list). But she wasn't taking any chances, and cannily had not set foot on British soil since the story broke - as much to stay away from Pete as the police. She even flew her family out to join her in the States for Christmas rather than risk being in the same country as her former lover.

This policy may have worked very nicely for Kate Moss (especially after she issued a public apology for letting people down): one by one the sponsors returned to her, remembering that products and publicity go together perfectly well. But for Pete it was a personal and professional disaster. The effect on his mental state has been plain to see, but the musical fall-out is sadder still. Because while a bit of controversy shouldn't do an old punk rocker much harm, in this case the human story was so big the long-awaited Babyshambles record became just a footnote. All this 'malarkey', as the man himself put it, only served to show that 'Pete 'n' Kate' was still bigger than 'Pete and the band'.

Plus the band weren't exactly the perfect group of lads to hang around with if you're trying to quit drugs. Whereas former bandmate Carl cobbled together new act Dirty Pretty Things from old hands with pro experience,[22] the 'Shambles were a real Camden rabble - the kind of people your parole officer and even your drug dealer would tell you to steer well clear of. And the endless sycophants and hangers-on were even worse. A tour insider told The Mirror, 'They are a bunch of junkie no-hopers. The band themselves are great but some of the people who hang around are tossers.'

The album itself, **Down In Albion**, got a mixed reception when it finally emerged in the trail dust of the supermodel scandal. Some good songs but a lot of filler, seemed to be the consensus. Of the new material, only the Brit-nominated title track and witty aside 'La Belle et La Bete' stood out, alongside a lot of recycled demos and apparently unfinished pieces.

An equally qualified success was the band's new tour. The acclaimed **Newcastle Journal** commented:

> There aren't many who could prompt 2,000 people to turn up to a gig on the promise that they might show up. Welcome to the world of Pete Doherty folks... that's the reality when you buy a Babyshambles ticket.

Never mind excessive drug use, in purely practical terms the tour was being undermined by Pete's constant arrests and court appearances. In the period spanning December 2005 to February 2006, he would visit a police cell or a courtroom at an average rate of once a week, on charges relating generally to vehicles, assaults and drugs - with drugs always being the common denominator. This included two charges of driving under the influence in the run-up to Christmas, a 13-day stint in Pentonville in February, and most comically one day the previous month when he was arrested three times.[23] Every major drug was covered in his winter resume: cocaine, heroin, crack, morphine and skunk. Telling police brazenly, 'If you search my car I'm fucked.' His gold Jaguar had become a patrol car bullseye.

These lost weeks did at least provide some classic Pete moments. Like giving one judge the finger in January, then five weeks later, up in front of another, being told he was 'doing quite well' - despite having re-offended and tested positive in the interim. Asked on leaving court whether he was still on drugs, he replied 'What sort of question is that for a Tuesday morning?'

...It was Wednesday. Which was how the newspapers reported it - they don't credit junkies for sending up the gallery. But such classy clowning was not on the check list of those vetting him for a place among the musical greats. At the 2006 NME Awards, he only managed to pick up Sexiest Male - an award that amused the conservative press no end, but which served to underline Pete's now-familiar role as fashion icon, not poet. While new darlings Arctic Monkeys swept all before them, NME.com referred to his band's low-key performance only as 'the ghost of Christmas past', describing him coldly as 'last year's man Pete Doherty'. And while prison may have inspired Johnny Cash's finest records, all Pete left Pentonville with was a mournful ditty that went 'I see my true love/On a Rimmel advert' to the tune of Louis Armstrong's 'What A Wonderful World'.

Still, there is much in 2006 for Pete to be grateful for. The new opiate blockers in his system; QPR's survival from relegation; and a justice system seemingly determined to avoid giving him a long custodial sentence[24]. More miraculously, he is still alive. And, as he scrawled 'I Love Kate 4 Eva' in felt-tip on his untaxed Jaguar windscreen, there were the inevitable rumours: that he was motoring off - if only the police would let him - to rejoin a clean and repatriated-to-the-runway Kate at her Gloucestershire

hideaway. It would be a fairytale end to
a scummy story: perhaps fitting for a
minstrel who keeps his head in the
clouds and a princess who dips her snout
in the drug trough. The Albion will
never sail on course, but perhaps her
sad captain will yet have the last
laugh.

In fact, after he'd appeared at Thames
Magistrates on March 23, there was
chaos outside the court as Pete wearing
his trademark trilby kicked fitfully at
a few of the guttersnipes who traffic in
his problems and shouted, 'This is a
victory for Pete.'

The problem for Pete is like society generally the odd victory cannot win him the war against drugs. In fact, on both levels the war is unwinnable. Pete genuinely is in NA-speak 'an addictive personality'. When he was banged up in early 2005 he wrote:

'Even life without drugs has gotta be betta than this malarkey. Won't do it again honest guv... Oh yes you will Doherty and you know it.'

The number of times that just this year he has done it again is becoming a national joke. In fact, the joke is now part of the proof that our judges are hopelessly soft on crime. But things really went beyond the tolerance of even the 'Left-Liberal Establishment' (that is, conspiracy) on Friday May 28th when **The Sun** published pictures of him injecting heroin into

a comatose young groupie. This was the 'final straw' for 'sick idiot' Doherty who had now sunk from the gutter to the sewer in depravity. The next day, the **Daily Mail** got in the act with running headline that except for naming the jail he should be in summed it all up: 'We Apologise to Readers Who Find These Pictures, and the Account That Goes With Them, Offensive. But We Believe They and Their Children Need to Know the Truth About Pete Doherty, Pop Star Lover of Kate Moss, Junkie, Criminal... And Hero of the Oh-so Liberal Media'. It was all absolutely disgusting and the only place for Pete was behind bars.

By the time **The Mail** had got in a lather of course, Pete was completely out of it

on the gear that the selling the story had gleaned. That night he put up on his website his blast against **The Sun**: 'Just a note to note the unjust Sun's disturbing and ridiculously offensive "story". Firstly, the photos are stolen from my flat so...upsetting and personally catastrophic...how rude, secondly it's a staged shot and what a fucking liberty to suggest I'd bang up a sleeping lass. Darkness.' The website is balachadha.com which mean 'good white', slang for crack. The cover for the scam was Pete's blood paintings, the paint for which he syringes from his own and his friends' veins. These oddball daubs can also now be bought for a grand a pop from the same website. However, the story got the boys in blue out in their patrol cars: they nicked Pete in an off-licence on the Saturday for 'recklessly administ- ering a noxious substance'. But on the Sunday he was released without charge. Next out came a right motley crew of ex-junkie rock'n'roll social workers, including Ozzie Osbourne, Elton John, 'Pedo' Pete Townsend, offering him help to get off drugs.

In March a reporter asked whether his drug habit was a death wish and he replied: 'Absolutely not. I don't take drugs to deaden me, I take 'em cos I love 'em. I know they're bad for my health, financially crippling and I'm an addict. But to me drugs are what I enjoy.' Meanwhile, between regular appearances before M'Lud, Kate still calls him 'my only love' and the readers of **NME**, which disses Pete as 'just a worn-out drug addict', named him the second greatest rock hero of all time.

It was an ominous listing: Kurt
Cobain was first and Morrissey,
who for years has been part of the
walking dead, was third.

We're all on borrowed time. It's
just that Pete borrows his at a
prohibitive rate of interest -
smack takes the highest dues.
Pete's the high-end of junkie
rock: yet Keith Richards is still
alive... just.

I see paint-cracked walls
stained with shite
Long long lock-up days
Cold lonely nights
And I think to myself ...
what a wonderful world
I see men touching fists
Saying "watcha bruv"
Screams from below
Shit parcels from above
And I think to myself ...
I see my true love
On a Rimmel advert.

footnotes

1 The rebels' progress; how Britain's most notorious acts climbed the charts:

Rolling Stones:
First single release Come On, July 1963
UK No.1 Album The Rolling Stones, April 1964
UK No.1 Single It's All Over Now, June 1964

Sex Pistols:
First single release Anarchy in the UK, November 1976
UK No.2 Single God Save the Queen, May 1977 (though widely perceived as a rightful No.1 single, after an alleged chart-fix saw Rod Stewart benefit from an unaccountable last-minute sales leap)
UK No.1 Album Never Mind the Bollocks Here's the Sex Pistols, October 1977

Oasis:
First single release Supersonic, April 1994
UK No.1 Album Definitely Maybe, August 1994
UK No.1 Single Some Might Say, April 1995

Libertines:
First single release What A Waster, June 2002 (like God Save the Queen 25 years before it, released to coincide with Jubilee week)
UK No.2 Single Can't Stand Me Now, August 2004
UK No.1 Album The Libertines, August 2004

2 Among UK acts Marti Pellow, once of Wet Wet Wet, stands as a dishonourable exception here - though his heroin problems did not emerge till long after the band's heyday. Of all the greats who have dabbled with heroin, in the modern age no-one else has made their habit a public talking point prior to their music.

3 BBC Collective interview, 17th October 2003

4 The **NME** would later attempt to redress the balance, most notably in their famous 'Pete or Carl' double-headed edition 2 years later.

5 **NME**, 22nd August 2002

6 Fashionfollower.com, May 2003

7 BBC Collective interview, 23rd July 2004

8 The second session also saw work begin on eventual album track Last Post on the Bugle

9 'Yes, I adored him. Yes, I was in love with him. But I was very let down.' – Panorama interview, November 1995, asked if she was unfaithful with James Hewitt. The two quotes have the same cadence, the same victim's tone in confession. Considering some 22.8m saw the interview it is quite possible Doherty on some level borrowed his PR act from the 20th century's arch-victim.

10 Rough Trade had first tried to have a Babyshambles meeting with Doherty back in July, but that agenda was overtaken by the more pressing concern of setting up his (abortive) rehab at Farm Place.

11 Originally written about on-off girlfriend and drug buddy Katie Bapples, it was later to be cynically hijacked when he presented the lyrics to a less buxom, but much more famous Katie.
12 As told to Pete Welsh in **Kids In The Riot**, Omnibus Press 2005

13 **The Sun**, 28th March 2004

14 The latter ran a story almost every day during the summer-autumn silly season, calling him variously a 'prat' and a 'junkie'. Although he never forgave that word, he was later to start co-operating with the paper.

15 Kate's birthday on January 16th had become an annual curtain-raiser for the hell-raiser. Her 30th the previous year had been a F. Scott Fitzgerald-themed extravaganza called The Beautiful and the Damned (sic). Never mind that this excuse for a 1920's knees-up was predicated on a misquotation, nobody in the media seemed to notice either.

16 Some Velvet Morning, 10th November 2003 (credited to: Kate Moss & Primal Scream)

17 He would go up to six months without seeing his daughter, although in fairness Moorish would back Doherty's desire to be more involved in her life when called upon to be a character witness in a court of law.

18 As told to Pete Welsh in **Kids In The Riot**, Omnibus Press 2005

19 Album The Libertines, August 2004

20 He has almost never had a bad word to say about Primal Scream, but by his own admission, 'Kate Moss singing on Some Velvet Morning was a mistake.' (poptones.co.uk interview, July 2004)

21 A half-touching, half-telling moment occurs towards the end, as the police arrive to break up the gig and ask who's responsible; both Pete and Carl point instinctively at each other.

22 Gary Powell and (Pete stand-in) Anthony Rossomondo from the Libs, plus Didz from defunct major-label hopefuls The Cooper Temple Clause.

23 January 26th 2006 – Driving under the influence, then an outstanding charge of assaulting a fan, then finally after being picked up by officers in possession while out on bail.

24 Pete's freedom is dependent on regular drug tests over the next year.